TOWARDS
WORLD
COMMUNITY

WORLD ACADEMY OF ART AND SCIENCE

5

TOWARDS WORLD COMMUNITY

edited by
JOHN NEF

1968
DR. W. JUNK N.V., PUBLISHERS - THE HAGUE

Telle est donc la condition humaine, que souhaiter la grandeur de son pays c'est souhaiter du mal à ses voisins. Celui qui voudrait que sa patrie ne fût jamais ni plus grande ni plus petite, ni plus riche ni plus pauvre, serait le citoyen de l'univers.

VOLTAIRE, *Dictionnaire Philosophique* ("Patrie").

Published for a Center for Human Understanding under the auspices of the American Division of the World Academy of Art and Science.

PRINTED IN HOLLAND BY KONINKLIJKE DRUKKERIJ VAN DE GARDE N.V., ZALTBOMMEL

Table of Contents

PART FOUR: THE PURSUIT OF BEAUTY

PART FIVE: SPECIALIZATION AND GENERAL CULTURE

PART SIX: ABOVE ALL NATIONS IS HUMANITY

APPENDIX

The Meeting in Session. From left to right: James Douglas, Lord Boyd Orr, Friedrich Hayek, Harold Rosenberg, Jacques de Bourbon Busset, John Nef, David Grene, Marshall Stone, Herbert Anderson, Madame de Bourbon Busset. Photograph by James Stricklin

Preface

A Center for Human Understanding was founded ten years ago within the flexible structure of the University of Chicago. It has sought to provide a meeting ground in which a few persons from many parts of the world, and from the realms of both thought and action, can learn from one another in an atmosphere where the search for truth is the paramount concern.

Independently of their particular callings and allegiances, but with the help of the experience these callings and allegiances provide, the participants have been pooling their knowledge in seeking alternatives to nuclear war. The present volume aims to communicate, to the public in all countries, the progress made in a series of sessions during a three-day meeting held in Chicago in October 1966.

This dialogue must be distinguished in a variety of ways from the myriad published reports of group conferences. Most of the contributors have known each other closely for years, and have met frequently, especially since 1962, for the discussion of matters relating to the search for world community.[1] They came to the Chicago meeting to listen as well as to talk, to develop their thought in relation to what others said. They aimed at coherence by dealing with a number of precise questions, formulated in advance through an executive committee consisting of Bourbon Busset, Morazé and myself, at repeated meetings in Europe from 1964 to 1966.

The principal characters in the dialogue took an active part in all the Chicago sessions. Their interest waxed as fresh themes were introduced. The discussion of these reveals new facets of subjects which were being explored, and suggests interrelations between those subjects.

So the book brings into a partial unity the thought of distinguished

1. For materials available concerning these earlier deliberations, see below, Appendix, p. 152

experts in many kinds of endeavor. Reading the dialogue, one is struck by the extent to which these experts succeed in communicating, out of their experience as specialists in very different domains,[1] not in the sense that they invariably agree but that their disagreements are constructive. Some of the disagreements lead towards reformulations of major questions which need to be answered in a search for world community.

The exchanges and the afterthoughts give the dialogue a living quality that makes it suitable for general reading. In the first five parts, the discussions are laid before the reader essentially as they came from the mouths of the participants at the time of the meeting. This places him in a position to examine for himself the subjects touched upon, to formulate questions and to form his own judgments.

In Part VI two of the witnessing participants, Lord Boyd Orr and the editor, set forth their views of the need for world community and the prospects of achieving it. Boyd Orr's observations were made on the last day of the Chicago conference and he has now rewritten them. Mine were written at the beginning of this year.

June 1, 1968.   JOHN NEF

---

1. Each participant has reviewed his own contribution or contributions as presented in these pages. His individuality has been respected. No effort has been made to impose on the contributions complete consistency in matters of capitalization, spelling, contractions, etc. It has seemed sufficient to maintain consistency in these matters within each individual's intervention.

Acknowledgments

In preparing this dialogue for publication I had the advantage, at an early stage, of advice from the Honorable James H. Douglas when, with our wives, we were on a brief tour which took us in March 1967 to Egypt, Athens and Vienna. Those who have known Mr. Douglas at any stage of his interesting and constructive life will have an inkling of the helpful part he played in selecting what to publish. He is one of the wise men of our time, with a genius for friendship from which I have benefitted again and again for almost sixty years.

The text was derived partly from prepared papers, partly from tapes on which were recorded the entire proceedings of the sessions in the Center for Continuing Education at the University of Chicago in October 1966. These tapes were admirably transcribed for my use by Miss Linnea Brandwein, a student of the Committee on Social Thought. The papers and the interventions, as edited, were submitted to the authors for correction. I am most grateful for their response. It has much improved the book.

My editorial work has been lightened by the assistance of Mrs. Jane Rohan, formerly secretary of a Center for Human Understanding, and in Chicago by that of Mrs. A. Armour, secretary for a quarter century of the Committee on Social Thought.

In preparing my contribution I have had the skillful help of my wife, Evelyn Stefansson Nef. She has eased and made delightful every inch of my way. Since we met early in 1964, I have come to find it impossible to think of any part of myself without her.

Dr. Stuart Mudd, Chairman of the Publications Committee of the World Academy of Art and Science, has increased our confidence in the value of this work, by inviting us to publish it under the auspices of the American Division of the World Academy of Art and Science.

Characters in the Dialogue

(In the order of their first intervention)

Marshall H. Stone, mathematician, Andrew MacLeish Distinguished Service Professor and Member of the Committee on Social Thought of the University of Chicago.

Samuel Devons, physicist, Chairman of the Department of Physics at Columbia University.

Herbert L. Anderson, physicist, Professor of Physics and formerly Director of the Enrico Fermi Institute of Nuclear Studies of the University of Chicago, Member of the Center for Human Understanding.

Rafael Squirru, poet and man of letters, Director of Cultural Relations in the Pan American Union. Author *Poesia (1957–1966)*.

Joseph P. Evans, neurological surgeon, Director of the Division of Neurological Surgery of the University of Chicago.

James H. Douglas, lawyer, Partner in Gardner, Carton, Douglas, Children & Ward; formerly Secretary of the Air Force and Deputy Secretary of Defense; Member of the Center for Human Understanding.

Friedrich A. Hayek, economist and social philosopher, Professor of Economics University of Freiburg, formerly Professor of Social and Moral Science in the Committee on Social Thought of the University of Chicago and Member of the Center for Human Understanding. Author *The Constitution of Liberty*.

Charles Morazé, historian, Professor in the Ecole Polytechnique, in the Institut d'Etudes Politiques and in the University of Paris, Member of the Center for Human Understanding. Author of *Essai sur la civilisation d'occident, La Logique de l'histoire*.

Marshall G. S. Hodgson, Islamic scholar and student of world history, Chairman of the Committee on Social Thought in the University of

Chicago. Author of *Venture of Islam: Conscience and History in a World Civilization.*[1]

DAVID GRENE, Classical scholar and student of the theatre, Professor in the Committee on Social Thought of the University of Chicago.

YU-SHENG LIN, Graduate student of Chinese civilization in the Committee on Social Thought of the University of Chicago, now at the University of Virginia.

HAROLD ROSENBERG, art critic and historian, art critic of *The New Yorker* Magazine and author of *The Anxious Object*, Professor in the Committee on Social Thought of the University of Chicago.

JACQUES DE BOURBON BUSSET, man of letters, former Chef de Cabinet to Foreign Minister Robert Schuman and Director of Cultural Relations in the French Foreign Office. Author of *La grande Conference, Le Protecteur.* Member of the Center for Human Understanding.

BERTRAND SCHWARTZ, engineer, Director of l'Ecole des Mines et de la Metal-lurgie de Nancy, of the Centre Universitaire de Cooperation Economique et Sociale, and of the Institut National pour la Formation des Adultes.

WILLIAM WOOD PRINCE, businessman and executive, Chairman, Armour & Company. Member of the Center for Human Understanding.

HERMON DUNLAP SMITH, insurance company executive and former Chair-man Marsh & McLennan. Member of the Center for Human Under-standing.

BOYD ORR, 1st Baron of Brechin, physiologist, Chancellor Glasgow Uni-versity, Nobel Peace Prize, and first President World Academy of Art and Science.

JOHN U. NEF, historian, founder of the Committee on Social Thought and Chairman Center for Human Understanding of the University of Chica-go. Author of *War and Human Progress, The United States and Civilization.* Fellow World Academy of Art and Science.

---

1. Marshall Hodgson died suddenly of a heart attack before this book of his appeared, and while *Towards World Community* was in process of publication.

PART I: THE EXPERIMENTAL SCIENCES

1. The Way to Utopia

by

MARSHALL H. STONE

We are here, I take it, to talk about Utopia – a world free from want, suffering and strife. In general, the sponsorship of this conference suggests that the way to such a world lies through human understanding. Today, in particular, we are to consider whether – and in what manner – the scientific enterprise can bring us closer to some ideal world of our own design. If this be possible through some scientific contribution to the betterment of human understanding, then we may hope in these discussions to define that contribution more closely. But if science should offer other means of finding a way to Utopia, that too should be made explicit in our conclusions.

Custom, I suppose, would have the first paper at such a conference as this sound the keynote and state the theme of a symphony that is about to be composed. At the very least the opening remarks would normally be expected to inspire and encourage, if not pointedly exhort, the participants to undertake their labors with both enthusiasm and self-confidence. If this be so, then I must honor custom mainly in the breach, for I am pessimistic about the role of human understanding in these matters, and skeptical about most of the proposals for building our Utopia upon an allegedly scientific foundation.

These feelings of mine are certainly not exceptional, for I share them with many another. Our times are times of gnawing doubt and pessimism. They are no times in which men naively or easily take into their hearts idealism or the urge to build an ideal world, however much they yearn for it. They are not times in which those who proclaim their idealism or their dedication to some noble cause are always worthy of belief, or find it a simple matter, even when they are, to win the confidence of their fellow-men. In literary and philosophical circles it is the day of the anti-hero and the existentialist. To be sure, the seventy-five years since the foundation of the University of Chicago have taught us hard, bitter lessons in almost every field of human endeavor. We have seen ancient principles, great landmarks, and time-honored institutions crumbled and all but swept away by the winds of change. Our past enthusiasms are now burnt out and it is difficult to kindle new ones on the ashes of the old. Even if we have somehow managed to preserve our faith in man's ultimate achievement of his more idealistic goals, we are nevertheless crushed by the immensity of the labor this is now seen to require and confused as to how we might best set our hands to the task.

In comparison with our twentieth century, the nineteenth seems to have been a time of greater hope and greater self-confidence. Utopian goals were not then thought of as entertaining fantasies or artificial conceits in terms of which to criticize the imperfections of the existing order, they were considered as something at which man might reasonably grasp and which, as the result of a little effort and persistence, he might soon successfully seize. At the end of the nineteenth century, the edifice of physical science, founded on mathematics and logic, seemed already so close to perfection that only a few finishing touches would be needed to bring it to a trium-phant completion. Although the political and economic institutions of that century were admitted to fall short of perfection, even in the more advanced countries, it seems to have been felt that the major imperfections and their first causes had been identified and could rather easily be elimi-nated by modifying the politico-economic structure in quite specific ways. Either by legislation or by revolution, it was claimed, an ideal society could be attained in a matter of decades.

The diagnoses of the ills of the body politic announced by the liberals, the Fabian socialists, and the Marxists were, of course, widely different, and so were the remedies they separately prescribed. That their optimism as to the prognosis was contagious is proved by the wide-spread acceptance of their doctrines in one form or another, both then and now.

Our century has put all these theories to the test, and an objective or dispassionate observer can only say that the results have been far from an unqualified success. In the field of physical science, the first thirty years of the present century have seen the theoretical edifice constructed by the nineteenth almost completely demolished and a start made toward re-placing it by a new structure resting on new foundations. And as though that were not sufficiently disturbing, the same period saw even the sup-posedly solid bases of mathematics and logic dealt shattering if not irrepar-able blows. In the fields of economics and politics, the claims of the liberals and socialists were seen to have been exaggerated or worse. The more extreme and far-reaching these claims, the more unrealistic they have proved to be. The most extreme claims and proposals, of course, were those put forward by the anarchists on the one hand and by the communists on the other. The communists described and promised a Utopian society which would demand from each citizen performance according to his capabilities and give him rewards based upon his needs. During the present century they succeeded in introducing in many lands the politico-economic constitutions they had prescribed as the sole and certain means for attaining this Utopia. In none of these countries does the actual state of society resemble even in outline the promised Utopia. The political chiefs in most of the communist countries have even given up the pretense that they are striving toward the Marxist Utopia and are tentatively seeking unorthodox or non-Marxian ways to better the poorly functioning economies of their states. Even the diplomacy of the nineteenth century, which, without having any Utopian pretensions, had envisaged a stable balance of power in Europe and a benevolent condominium of European nations over the rest of the world, produced disaster, marked by two of the bloodiest and most destructive holocausts since the Thirty Years' War and the total collapse of the power system it had sought to perpetuate.

Despite these tremendous failures and their profound, well-nigh traumatic effect upon mankind, we must clearly recognize the courage and the high sense of purpose displayed by the first generation that ever undertook consciously and in all seriousness to translate an ideal world order into reality. Out of the many bitter frustrations in which their hopes and ours have foundered, it would be wrong to distill only a cynical doctrine of defeatism and despair. The lesson we have had to learn is that bettering the condition of mankind, even in some quite modest way, is an infinitely more complicated and difficult task than our fathers and grandfathers appear to have believed – a task requiring deeper knowledge, greater astuteness, and more lasting patience than have yet been brought to bear upon it.

These, at least, are the grounds for the pessimism and skepticism I have expressed earlier in my remarks. There is little justification for thinking that human understanding will prove to be a better solvent for man's political or economic ills than it has been in the past. History is replete with accounts of situations that seemed to offer every opportunity for human understanding to avert tragedy but ended nevertheless in murder, civil strife, or war. At every level of human existence it is almost a truism that the closest neighbors can become the bitterest enemies. Within the framework of European culture and tradition warfare between peoples has been nearly incessant: over the centuries Frenchman has been pitted against German, Englishman against Frenchman, and German against Slav. Indeed, it does not seem to me that understanding between men is really difficult to achieve, even when important differences in culture and tradition appear to stand in the way. But understanding is not necessarily a strong enough psychological factor to control other powerful human motives. One does not have to subscribe to the Marxian thesis of the economic determination of history to recognize that economic motives are among them. In short, human behavior is always the result of a conflict among psychological forces upon the outcome of which we have at present no really effective means of exerting a favorable influence. Historically religion has not been able to exert such an influence, and in the present state of our knowledge science can hardly be expected to do so either. What we have observed in our times and are likely to witness in the immediate future is a potent, but nevertheless clearly indirect, influence of science and technology in man's struggle towards a better social and international order.

Through applications of the physical and biological sciences man has wrought profound and far-reaching changes in the use he can make of the material resources available to him and in many aspects of his daily life. The banishment of want has been made possible by science, in the sense that theoretically and technically we know how to reach and maintain a satisfactory equilibrium between supply and demand in many areas of human consumption. Physics has transformed the nature of warfare through the introduction of atomic or nuclear weapons. There is no doubt that the existence of concentrated military power based on stores of these weapons held in readiness has served to prolong an uneasy peace in the face of provocations and conflicts that would have resulted under earlier circumstances in open warfare. War involving the use of nuclear weapons appears far less profitable than its prenuclear forms were once thought by statesmen to be. War between nuclear powers can hardly be considered as an effective means of securing their conflicting national interests. In this manner science has indirectly made war less likely by making it more terrible and destructive. In yet another way, also indirect, science has contributed to the devaluation of war as an instrument of national policy, namely by increasing the mutual dependence of national economies upon one another, through improvements in communications and the multiplication of technical involvements between industries in different lands. From these examples we may perhaps be allowed to infer a general principle to the effect that science may alter the conditions of human existence to such an extent that men will be forced consciously to alter their behavior in an effort to adapt themselves to those new conditions. It is not inconceivable that eventually war might thus disappear simply because men had come to fear it enough to create some effective kind of world federation – and this without any preliminary increase in human understanding or the eventual elimination of bitter political struggles among conflicting interests around the world.

In these terms, then, science is viewed as a blind, albeit powerful, influence shaping a new but unpredictable world order. It is superposed upon other and equally blind forces which have always been at work in human affairs. In my reading of Tolstoy's "War and Peace," I understand him to be saying, among other things, that for all his genius Napoleon, in company with other men of his time, was more the tool of such forces than an independent agent in his own right. In any case, we must be candid in admitting that we are not in a position either as men or as scientists to foresee, guide, or control the full impact of scientific discoveries upon mankind. The most diverse experiences make this abundantly clear. To illustrate by yet another example, drawn from the field of biology, I need only remind this audience of certain consequences of the introduction of antibiotics – rapid and, in some regions, alarming increases in population, and the emergence of resistant strains of dangerous microorganisms. These consequences are disturbing enough that decisions to control in certain ways the use of antibiotics may have to be taken. In general this need for some kind of guideline for a more rational exploitation of our scientific knowledge is ever more keenly felt by reflective men and women the world over. There are at least two reasons why a satisfactory response to this need is hard to find. One is that it would probably involve many political decisions which would be difficult to make and enforce within the existing social structure. The other is our inability as scientists to predict with any great accuracy or certainty the developments we would seek to control.

Thus we must look to an increase of both knowledge and wisdom if we desire to render science significantly more helpful in the construction of our Utopia. I believe that science can and will contribute to the needed increase in basic knowledge, especially in the field of human biology and human behavior. I believe that important and perhaps startling discoveries in these fields will be made before the first century of this University has run its course – and I hope that some of them may be made within its walls. I shall not attempt to spell out these possibilities in detail, as I can safely leave them to the imagination of my hearers. Wherever imagination points the way, surprising facts are likely to be turned up by courageous investigators – though not necessarily just the ones which have been forecast or anticipated. Indeed, it is not hard to imagine a world in which our capabilities for the direction and control of human behavior will have been vastly enhanced. We already have in hand some of the tools required – electronic computers with which to handle the massive data involved, the beginnings of a science of cybernetics and the control of interacting systems, the rudimentary techniques for shaping personality through psychological and physicochemical interventions. Nor is it hard to foresee that in such a world effective planning could become a reality – but a reality involving extensive social controls and a restriction of personal liberties from which we instinctively recoil. These prospects have the power to terrify, and thoughtful writers such as Aldous Huxley and Orwell have felt this power and have sought to warn us in some of their novels of the dangers ahead. I have no doubt that they are right in telling us how through scientific advances we are being carried along the path of increasing co-ordination and integration of human society and how in such a society the problems of power and human folly may be magnified many fold. For a highly articulated and tightly organized social structure involves the concentration of immense power in the hands of a relatively few, endowed with sufficient knowledge to manipulate public opinion in the interest of their planning.

Thus at the very heart of our inquiry we again come face to face with one of the most ancient of human problems – the problem of power. If there be a single root of all evil, it must surely be the desire for power. For this desire works in each of us, sometimes openly but quite often in hidden ways; it feeds upon all our other desires, simply because a ready means to their satisfaction is offered by power over other men, and it swells rather than declines with the acquisition of its coveted object. The desire for power thus engenders infinite conflict and strife, while the exercise of power all too often corrupts and perverts those who wield it. Yet an adequate social order is inseparable from the conferral of great power upon selected leaders, so that the most ambitious and power-hungry are tempted and the seeds of its own corruption are nurtured by the very measures adopted for its creation and maintenance. In the nature of things, the problem of power thus confronts men with a dilemma that can neither be removed nor definitely resolved – and least of all is it a dilemma that can be removed by science. The only way we have of dealing with this great eternal problem is to search without pause for some sort of more or less satisfactory compromise based upon an ingenious system of checks and balances. Perhaps science will provide us from time to time with new means for extending and improving this system – for example, by enabling us to identify more certainly those to whom great power should be denied or to prescribe for the chosen wielders of power conditions conducive to the wise and benevolent discharge of their functions. However, when all is said and done, the only ultimate check upon the exercise of great power lies in great self-restraint. It may be that a Utopian order might be established by the ruthless and unrestrained exercise of power; but no Utopia can be founded on ignorance of the nature of man and none can long survive without the intervention of self-restraint. If you would find a way to Utopia, therefore, my parting injunction to you is not "Know thy neighbor" but "Oh, Man, know thyself."

2. Limitations of the Teaching of Science

by

Samuel Devons

Professor Stone warns us, I think rightly, against being over-enthusiastic as to what science can achieve. He is much more involved that I am in human and social affairs, so I am going to comment briefly, not so much from the point of view of the scientist per se, as from that of a teacher of science, teaching directed not exclusively to scientists but to students in general.

I start with what I own is a very melancholy fact about education, namely that it is the province of the old, the ageing, based upon past experience, to teach the young about what to do in the future. One consequence of this strange situation is that the young resent it. I don't believe that in teaching, particularly in teaching science to young people, one is ever trying to solve their problems. These are *their* problems, not our problems, that they are interested in, and their problems will be different from ours. I think I echo some of the sentiments of Mr. Stone in saying that we, in this generation, cannot solve the next generation's problems. The only big problem we can perhaps help to solve is that there should *be* a next generation, with its own problems.

What relation is there between this and the teaching of science as I see it, teaching which tries to impart some of the lessons of science, particularly to people who are not professionally concerned with science?

I will not dwell on the obvious achievements of science, the material achievements that are a consequence of science. I think one tends in the teaching of science to overemphasize achievements and success – not that they are not there, but I think one tends to overemphasize and stress them almost to the exclusion of a completely different aspect of science and a different lesson which we forget – namely its limitations and restrictions and the inability to forecast its consequences, which Professor Stone has mentioned.

This inability of ours to forecast the consequences of science has at least two aspects. First, there is the inability to forecast the course of scientific development itself. The best established, the finest theories some day meet their doom. Secondly, we are even more uncertain about the social and the technological consequences, of any scientific development, even a single generation ahead. This combination of achievement, of success, in science with its weaknesses and limitations, can provide a very valuable object lesson. The enormous evidence on which many a scientific theory is based, the great scrutiny with which it is examined, the detailed analysis and verification which follows, lead one easily to the conclusion that one has arrived at the truth. If one compares such an apparent truth with, say, many an utterance that is made (often by scientists themselves) about a social phenomenon, or about political events, one is struck by the lack of certainty, the obscurity, the difficulties. These contrast sharply with the apparent certainty of a scientifically established statement.

Yet even in the most well attested, the most thoroughly and the most exhaustively analyzed scientific concept, there is often a fault at the base. There are misinterpretations, there is some complete lack of understanding which only succeeding generations can find. So if, in the domain of the sciences themselves (the so-called "exact" sciences), one must retain a spirit of modesty, how much more is this essential in dealing with the vastly more complicated problems of social phenomena and evolution, of the consequences of scientific discoveries for society. This rather paradoxical mixture of lack of understanding with triumphant understanding provides a lesson of the first importance for human understanding. This is one of the things which I think the natural sciences can teach us.

I would like to comment on just one other aspect of Dr. Stone's paper. This is the question of trying to determine the future, of trying to map Utopia. I don't believe myself that the issue has changed in quite the way he put it, at least not with the present generation of young people whom I meet. It's not that the old utopias have proved false and have given way to new ones. It is rather that nobody thinks in terms of utopias any more. There is no belief in such a thing as utopia, and most people believe that if a utopia were found and arrived at, it would be deadly boring. The purpose of the analysis of social problems, it seems to me, is not to achieve particular goals, but to avoid particular disasters. So, in relation to Stone's question of the extent to which technology has, perhaps by accident, removed the likelihood of war, there again I think one must be extremely cautious about evaluating this achievement, because all wars are not alike, all disasters are not alike. The problem is not simply to avoid all disasters equally; one should rather look for the probability of disaster and multiply it by the magnitude of the disaster. Magnitude is the effective measure of what one has to avoid. And there it is not at all obvious that the advent of, let us say, atomic or nuclear technology, has improved the situation.

I think this notion of not trying to determine the future, not being able to determine the future, and also not wanting to determine the future, has its counterpart to one's approach in education. Again I am talking particularly about scientific education. Our purpose in scientific education, or perhaps I should say my purpose in scientific education, is not so much to impart knowledge as to eradicate ignorance. By ignorance I do not mean lack of knowledge, but positive ignorance, crass ignorance, prejudice, stupidity, cant, humbug. While the vital problems may not be solved by intelligence, it seems to me much less likely that they will be solved by ignorance and prejudice. And science can in fact distinguish between crass ignorance and what I might call modest ignorance, a sense of the limitations of one's understanding and one's knowledge, a certain modesty in the face of tremendous problems. Such modesty is not equivalent to ignorance. In fact, there is an old adage, I think it comes from the Ethics of the Fathers, that he knows who knows that he knows not, because he knows that he knows not. And that is one of the things that science teaches us. I think this lesson of science is particularly apt for social phenomena. That is, there is a limit to what one can teach, and there is a limit to what one can predict. One cannot formulate, still less create, a utopia, but one can eradicate ignorance and this can help us to avoid disaster.

3. Science in the Defence of Human Dignity

by

Herbert Anderson

It is well to recognize, as Professor Stone has done, the gravity of the problems now connected with human survival, and to realize, as Professor Devons has indicated we should, the limitations of our attempts to solve these problems. I think it is true that we will never develop a complete understanding such as would enable us to predict with some measure of certitude what will be the consequences of our actions.

Yet I like to think that the development of science in recent times should perhaps give us some courage by the example of its own success. For the physicist this has meant the solution of a great many mysteries. We have now arrived at clear explanations of the behavior of atoms, molecules, electrons, nuclei. The discoveries in the pure sciences during the late '20s and early '30s brought about a great surge of scientific development and understanding, particularly in physics. Physicists, and I think scientists in general, developed a sense of sureness and conviction. In spite of the limitations of their knowledge, they felt they now knew enough so that they could plan their work with conviction and sureness. This had important historical consequences when the Western world was threatened by a Nazi invasion. The stage was set by the impressive advances which had taken place in physics. The call went out and the physicists responded with radar, with proximity fuses, with rockets, with computers, and then with nuclear bombs. They were able to do this, because they knew how, they knew what they were able to do, and they had convictions about their understanding. They were able to save the Western world as we know it from the destruction of human values which the Nazis threatened.

The Second World War gave science a new type of recognition. It was recognized as essential for national survival, and it also became and was recognized as a principal instrument for dealing with human problems, the basic human problems of food and shelter, of health and well being, and beyond this of the opportunity and the freedom to enjoy the interests and pleasures that a good life can provide. One of its contributions, as we realize now, is the virtually limitless supply of energy which is essential if we are to have material plenty. This is a development which came out of the war, and which we have in hand today. Atomic energy plants are now economically advantageous, and of the power plants, which are now on the drawing boards and are being planned for construction in the immediate future, forty percent are of the nuclear energy variety.

The electronic computer also had its beginnings during the war. It has brought with it an associated technology which has vastly increased our capacity to solve difficult technical problems, such as the problem of handling vast numbers of objects in the economic and social fields. It has greatly increased the efficiency with which we can muster our technical resources toward directed ends.

The new level of technical efficiency provides us with a certain excitement and a certain incentive toward the achievement of world community. But, at the same time, this new level of technical efficiency has created new dangers. The advances in science and technology have not been matched by comparable advances in social and political relations. If people feel they are sufficiently threatened, they are still disposed to resort to the use of any and all means of destruction available, and science has provided means, far more devasting than were ever before, at the service of violence.

We could solve the technical problems of providing a comfortable human life, if only we were able to manage the concomitant, much more difficult and less understood social, economic and political problems.

Science sets another example for community of action. In the realm of pure science, we have a long history of the easy exchange of ideas and information across national frontiers. In the early history of modern physics, one can mention the names of Galilei, an Italian, Kepler, a German, and Gilbert, an Englishman, all in one breath. There was a very close exchange of information between them.

Later we come on examples of the exchange of scientific information between countries which were actually at war with one another. During the eighteenth and early nineteenth centuries, French and English men of science were allowed safely to cross each other's national borders though they were politically and militarily enemy lines. It was also in this era that Sir Humphrey Davy received an award from the French government while his country was at war with France. Benjamin Franklin, during the American Revolution, requested American naval ships and privateers to grant the vessels of Captain Cook safe passage because of the scientific nature of Cook's expedition to the South Seas and the Antarctic.

Today we have many more instances of the cooperation that a common interest in science engenders, and we recognize the fact, the University of Chicago recognizes it, that science, at any rate, develops best if there is a free and a complete exchange of information. We have many international meetings. Someone has estimated that during this last year some 20,000 American scientists have met with 60,000 or 80,000 from other nations at some 2,000 international meetings. This indicates the way that the development of science opens avenues to world understanding.

I thought you would be interested in some examples of that sort of thing. I attended this summer some three international conferences, and at one of them I heard an interesting talk by Dr. Glenn Seaborg, presently the chairman of the U.S. Atomic Energy Commission, in which he brought together a number of cases in which there had been international collaboration of an encouraging variety. One of these, in my own field, with which I am quite familiar and with which Bourbon Busset had a great deal to do in its early days,[1] is the Center for Nuclear Research in Geneva (CERN) in which some thirteen Western European countries participate. The main reason is that in my field of research the apparatus is extremely large and extremely expensive. The countries of Europe each individually felt that they couldn't afford to spend that much money. So they pooled their resources to their mutual advantage.

That Center has been enormously successful. It has been in existence ten years now, and has provided, I think it's fair to say, a tremendous impetus for the scientific development of all thirteen countries, first by presenting young men, who are coming up in the universities in various parts of Europe, the kind of opportunities for doing research that they felt they ought to have but which earlier they could not have had without immigrating to the United States. By developing the CERN center they were able to stay in Europe and to carry through their scientific education and then return to their own countries and encourage other young men to continue the work.

Another example is a new center that was established by the International Atomic Energy Agency, an international center for theoretical physics at Trieste. This was the first scientific research institution to be established under the sponsorship of the United Nations. The objectives are international cooperation, emphasis on the role of the developing countries,

1. Cf. below, pp. 91-92

and the advancement of theoretical physics. It was generally agreed when the idea for the center was first raised, that theoretical physics offered the most fruitful field of inquiry since work of a high order in that area had been done by scientists from a number of developing countries, and it had the advantage, by focusing on theoretical physics, which could be studied on an advanced level in many of the developing countries, that it could be established with a minimum of expense for providing laboratories. All too often, scientists from the developing countries had been obliged after completing research in one of the scientifically advanced countries, either to leave their own country, or to live there in virtual scientific hibernation. Now such a scientist can come to the center for a stay as a fellow or an associate and meet some of the outstanding minds from many countries, in his own and in closely related fields, without having to cut his home ties.

Another extremely interesting organization is the International Council of Scientific Unions, the ICSU, which is the parent organization of the International Union of Pure and Applied Physics. The success of the ICSU attests the value of the cross-fertilization of scientific ideas. There are fifty-four member countries, and one of the outstanding examples of the ICSU is its project, a number of years ago, called International Geophysical Year, which ultimately involved sixty-six nations. The International Geophysical Year itself was highly successful, and one of its offspring, the Indian Ocean Expedition, which comprises twenty-five nations, studies that body of water which covers some fourteen percent of the surface of the earth.

In the investigation of solar-terrestrial relationships sixty countries cooperated in what was called the International Year of the Quiet Sun. And another interesting development is that during the International Geophysical Year, an antarctic research program was organized whereby twelve nations, including the United States and the Soviet Union, agreed by treaty to reserve the Antarctic for thirty years solely for scientific research. During this time all territorial claims on any part of this vast continent will be held in abeyance.

Another activity under the ICSU is the World Meteorological Association, in which there are 126 member nations, and they are planning a world weather watch. In the near future, this may make it possible to receive daily forecasts as much as two weeks in advance, and further the goals of large-scale weather modification and control. Toward this end, two World Meteorological Centers have been established, in Washington and in Moscow, and a third is to be established in Melbourne, Australia.

These world-wide research programs attest to another fact of life concerning scientific investigation today. For much of our research the entire earth – its land, the ocean, atmosphere, all of its life – becomes the laboratory, the source of investigation. Therefore national boundaries have to be overlooked. I think this is an encouraging sign.

The latest research project to be coordinated by the ICSU is the International Biological Program, in which there are forty-three nations cooperating in a world-wide study – organic production on land, and in fresh waters and the sea – in order to estimate how man can most effectively manage his environment.

We may talk about international cooperation in research, pure scientific research. But the impetus for the growth of most of our science today, I believe, springs not solely from the basic curiosity that man may have about his world, it springs from man's needs and from the belief, only recently engendered in our history, that science can radically better our lives here on earth. To this end, international efforts are going on in applied science and technology, and are making tremendous strides.

These efforts are really only beginning. What can and will be done in the future?

We all know that the production of sufficient food is a major problem in the world and is likely to become increasingly urgent. The problems of hunger in many areas require our immediate attention. A concerted effort under the United Nations Food and Agricultural Organization, called a freedom from hunger campaign, has been launched. It involves eighty countries working with UNICEF, UNESCO, the World Health Organization, the International Atomic Energy Agency, International Labor Organization, World Meteorological Organization. This combination of international scientific-educational groups is exploring every natural, technological, economic and social means for providing basic food staples for human beings everywhere.

Closely related to the world shortage of food is a scarcity of clean water. One of UNESCO's most significant programs confronted with this problem is the International Hydrological Decade. During the period 1965–1975 it is planned to establish a global network of stations to measure and track water in its cycle from rain to the underground water table and back to the atmosphere. In addition, studies concerned with the expansion of freshwater supplies are being carried on.

I should also mention, as a further example of international scientific cooperation in meeting the world's water problems, the First International Conference of Water for Peace scheduled to be held in Washington, D.C. The purpose of the Conference will be to report on the actions taken and the progress made in meeting man's need for pure water. It will represent a major expression of many nations to help each other scientifically, technically and economically, as well as a major effort to determine the current scientific and industrial capabilities of the world community in the developing conservation in the use of the world's water resources.

I think that, while recognizing the full weight of the difficulties and problems before us, we must nevertheless take some satisfaction, some pleasure if you will, that progress is being made in these directions. If the young men who succeed us want problems to solve, we have given them plenty. And we have given them, I think, some examples of how it is possible to reach solutions, not complete solutions, but how to solve little bits here and there. For many of us that is satisfaction enough.

Before ending this message for the oncoming generation of physical scientists, however, I return to the circumstances in connection with the Second World War in which the physicists of my generation have worked. We felt that human dignity was so threatened by the tyranny and armed expansion of Nazi Germany, we had no choice but to take the risks of putting all our knowledge and scientific resources at the service of the search after the most powerful means of destruction that it seemed theoretically possible to discover.

As I move years afterwards among my non-scientific friends, I am beginning to develop a guilt complex about having done what I did, and I am more conscious of this guilt because the University of Chicago has now celebrated the twenty-fifth anniversary of the first chain reaction. I don't know whether to be proud or ashamed of that event.

But I have to remind my good friends that we do not come into the world without encumbrances. We come with a certain history behind us. In my case, I came into the world as a graduate student when the Nazis were beginning to overrun Europe. They were threatening England, on the one hand, and possibly our own country, on the other. And we were faced with the shock of Pearl Harbor from the Japanese side. It seemed to me at that time there was a fire we had to put out before we could go on to higher things. As I have already pointed out, we physicists felt, and I felt as a young graduate student having become privy to the mysteries of my science, that we really had something with which we could work. The discovery of the fission process was immediately recognized as having the potential of unprecedented amounts of power.

I remember Professor Fermi, who was both my teacher and my mentor, discussed with me the advantage of carrying on some research in this field. He said: "if you work with me in this field, some day you'll be the president of the Uranium Corporation of America and you'll make lots of money." That interested me a lot! But it didn't work out that way. The war started, and our attention was turned away from the peaceful possibilities of atomic power to the possibilities of devising a new weapon. As a matter of fact, even that was not our initial interest. What we feared was that the Germans might recognize the possibilities of which we had become aware and develop it for their own not very gentle purposes. We did not have a peaceful arrangement with the people who were running Germany at that time! We were worried about what they might do to us, and we thought that the best course, if an atomic bomb were possible, was to make one ourselves first.[1] It could turn out that a chain reaction based on fission would not be possible. Some of us hoped that the neutron emission, which was essential in the working of the device, might by its nature be too small to permit a chain reaction. If it turned out that the neutron emission were very slow, it might be possible to have general power but not an explosion from the reaction. We did not know how it would turn out in the end but we did know how to study the problem and find out, and we thought that it was essential to do so.

Well, it turned out that the neutron emission was copious, and the neutron emission was very fast, and that it was possible to make an explosive device. Since the country was at war, and since many of our countrymen were involved and their lives were threatened, we went ahead and made our atomic bomb. And then, I remember, the question came up, at the very end, should it be used? There was actually at the University of Chicago a committee called the Franck Committee which discussed whether this was a wise thing to do, in view of what could happen to humanity later on. You must remember that, at the time the atomic bomb was nearing completion, Germany had already lost the war and given up, and we had only the final assault on Japan to carry out. The question was whether it was a good idea to expose this great weapon to the world view and horror or whether it would be better to put this weapon under some sort of wraps. This committee met and made a very serious attempt to persuade the Government not to use the atomic bomb. I have often wondered about the

1. This point of Mr. Anderson's should be stressed. The first participants in the experiment, which was destined to change the meaning of warfare, were prompted above all by their *fear* of Nazi Germany. Mr. Stone tells me that when the Germans were defeated in 1945 before the atomic bomb was ready, these participants (not a few of them refugees from the Nazi tyranny) lost interest in the project. But it was then too late to turn back (Ed.).

wisdom of using the atomic bomb to wipe out the two cities, Nagasaki and Hiroshima. The main reason for using the bomb was that, if it were not used, it would be necessary to carry through a major invasion of the Japanese mainland. The estimates were that some 100,000 or 200,000 American lives would be lost in that invasion, to say nothing of the loss of life in Japan. It was felt that it was necessary to do something, whatever was possible, to avoid that sacrifice.

The argument was made by the Franck Committee that a demonstration could be made which would show the Japanese leaders that the weapon we had at our disposal could be extremely destructive and thereby persuade them to give up and surrender. Well, the feeling was that this wouldn't work. I myself shared in that feeling because I was present at Alamagordo. I participated in the first atomic bomb experiment. When you see an atomic device explode in the desert, it's a very impressive sight. You see a flash, a large flash of very bright light. But I must say that it was only after the bomb went off and some measurements had been made about pressures and heat generation, that it was possible to make a prediction about the degree of destruction that would be wrought by such a bomb. No one at Los Alamos was persuaded that a demonstration would serve the purpose and that it would lead the Japanese leaders to immediate surrender.

An important point was that we had only one bomb. There was a good chance that it wouldn't go off at the test. We couldn't be sure. No one had ever tried something like this before. We like to believe that we can predict the course of an experiment but there is always an element of uncertainty. We couldn't be sure the bomb would go off. What if the whole demonstration were a flop?

I remember the pool that was organized at that time. Anyone could bet a dollar on the pool and enter his guess about the success of the bomb, how much energy would be released. The winner of the pool was Professor Rabi. His guess was the most optimistic of all. He said: "Of course it's going to work," and he submitted a high value for the energy released. Most of the others who participated guessed partial success or failure.

At the time of Hiroshima there were only two bombs available. It was considered very important to impress upon the Japanese leadership that things were really hopeless, that we had unlimited power of destruction. The President made the decision to go ahead.

There are two things to be said for this. First, it did terminate the war abruptly. The second point is probably more important. We know now that such weapons can be made. Was it better that everyone know this and have, from direct experience, a certain knowledge of its great devastating power? Or would it have been better to try keeping this knowledge concealed? There would then be the possibility that some country hostile to us would discover the bomb anew, for whatever advantage it might want to press.

We can take some comfort in the thought that ever since the awesome demonstration at Hiroshima and at Nagasaki some twenty long years ago, there hasn't been a single instance of either an atomic bomb or a hydrogen bomb, its even more impressive successor, exploded in anger.

4. A Human Chain Reaction

by

MARSHALL H. STONE

I believe I have something to add to what Mr. Anderson said, not because I worked on the bomb, but because I happen to know something about the way it was put into use.

In the first place, one matter of fact, which should always be remembered in the discussion of the use of the bomb against Japan, is that the United States Army Air Force was capable, without the use of the bomb, of producing equivalent destruction and it had already done so in Tokyo and Yokohama. In a single raid more than 100,000 people were killed in those two cities and a comparable area of the cities destroyed. So what was done in Hiroshima and what was done in Nagasaki could just as well have been done by other means.

It was therefore not a question of inflicting the destruction, but of inflicting the destruction by unusual means. Whether or not we should have done this is the question. My own feeling, based on a very intimate and close observation of what was happening in Japan at that time, was that we should not have done so. The reason for this was, first, that the Japanese were militarily incapable of carrying on, though capable of putting up strong resistance in the southern islands if invaded. They were themselves actively suing for peace. They had, by the time the bomb was experimentally exploded in Los Alamos, initiated moves to reach some kind of settlement with the United States. They used two methods to do this. One was to ask the Russian government, with which they were at peace, to present their request. And they also asked the Swiss government to do this. The Russian government never transmitted the Japanese request to the United States. The Swiss did.

From early summer the discussions were going on. The Japanese understandably were not prepared to accept the absolute unconditional surrender which was asked of them, and they stalled and tried to get some kind of negotiation. A time for using the atomic weapons experimentally and for military purposes in Japan was set already at the beginning of the summer. A date was chosen with a view to the meteorological conditions which would prevail over the two cities to be attacked, because it was desired to make some direct observations, and Japanese weather at that season was very uncertain. The best days were chosen with this in mind. The President of the United States, by virtue of the circumstances under which he took office, was uninformed about the existence and nature of the bomb and felt that he had to call on others for advice. He set up a special committee which studied this whole question and came to a decision after a review of all the circumstances, including the protest which came from the Franck Committee, which Mr. Anderson has described. On the presidential committee there sat at least one scientist, if I am not misinformed. I think Dr Vannevar Bush of MIT was a member of that committee. The committee examined everything and came to the conclusion that, in the light of all that was going on, it would be advantageous to use the bomb, that it might conceivably push the Japanese the last step toward accepting surrender and thus avoid the sacrifices which an invasion of Kyushu would have cost us.

There are many other factors that might have entered into that decision: the fact that we had spent an enormous amount of money and that in an open democratic society this would somehow have to be explained after the war was over. It would have been difficult for any administration to go to the people of the United States, saying that we had spent two billion dollars without anything material to show for it. Demonstration was necessary not only for the Japanese but also for the Americans, if this point of view was taken.

But this is not the most important thing I want to say. I think the really important thing that needs to be said about this whole experiment with atomic and nuclear energy is that the scientists not only studied a physical chain reaction but they initiated a human chain reaction. I think that Mr. Anderson's own arguments about this whole question, his reasons for thinking at the time and now that it was desirable to build a bomb and to make use of it at the critical moment, illustrate exactly the mechanism of the chain reaction which I shall talk about in the last minutes of this intervention.

We built the bomb. Its existence became known to other powers. The Russians certainly knew it through espionage, though they were not invited during the war to participate in its construction in the United States. Thus the Russians were faced with the problem: should they or should they not build comparable weapons. They thought, correctly, that they had the scientific capability. They had available knowledge such as was divulged with great generosity by the United States in the Smythe Report published just the day the war ended. They had to take into account the situation of Russia vis-a-vis the rest of the world, especially the United States. And they came to the decision, by arguments very much like those described by Mr. Anderson in connection with his participation in building a bomb and they came to exactly the same conclusion, that they should build their bomb. The best efforts of the United States at that time to secure through diplomatic channels the renunciation of the development and use of atomic weapons, came to nothing because the Russians were determined that they would have the weapon themselves. And this chain reaction is not over. Britain followed suit; France followed suit. There are other countries which would like to follow suit. The Chinese have now done so – this was to be expected. But we even have countries like Indonesia which in a moment of expansivity claimed that it would have *its* atomic bomb.

This kind of chain reaction does not result from any physical laws. It results from laws of human psychology. I do not see how we could expect people to act in any other way. So it is not just chain reactions that occur in the physical world – it is also chain reactions that occur in the human world which we have to deal with. And I am quite sure that this is not the last of such phenomena which will emerge because of new knowledge in the physical world. I think we can only anticipate – prudently, we *must* anticipate – the other things, perhaps in the realm of biological warfare, which may come up. These are just as terrible and perhaps more subtle and more far-reaching in their consequences than anything we have thought of in physics. So while it may help us to look backwards, I think we must realize that this is basically a human problem. It is not a problem that a physicist or a biologist can solve on the basis of his professional knowledge.

5. Nuclear Weapons and Human Survival

by

R AFAEL S QUIRRU

I should like to preface these remarks by acknowledging that the particular angle of my interest in Dr. Stone's opening paper bears an analogy to a recent remark of John Cage when, in listening to a concert of Mozart's music, he was arrested by a gesture of the musician playing the oboe. In the midst of the performance the musician chewed his oboe and spat. This "happening" became for Cage the key to the whole concert.

Similarly, I was arrested when Dr. Stone remarked, in an aside, "*In my reading* of Tolstoy . . ." He then went on to give *his* version of *War and Peace*. One might have expected Stone to say: "As we read in Tolstoy." But instead he took this shrewd way of letting us know he was giving us *his* interpretation.

Therefore in referring, as I now venture to do, to a scientist, working in a field completely outside my sphere of specialization, I must warn you that it is as *I* read Conrad Lorenz. This does not establish, by any means, that this is what Lorenz really says. In any case, I was very impressed by his book *On Aggression* that appeared in article form in the English magazine, *Encounter*.

He observes that man is now going through a very dangerous stage in his development. Biologically, he has reached a point where he can bring about destruction that is totally disproportionate to his physical equipment. I remember a comparison that impressed me very much, of what might happen if a dove suddenly found itself with the beak of an eagle. Would it be able to survive, would its species be able to survive?

We have suddenly discovered the use of atomic weapons. It isn't inbred in our instincts not to make use of them. Judging from an interview I saw some time ago on T.V., a leader of opinion, who has an influence on the political destiny of this country, was asked at one point whether atomic weapons should be used in the present conflict. He answered, "I do not preclude anything." In other words, they might be used.

So I think this is the moment to sober up and to start thinking whether, if science is a blind force, as could be deduced from Dr. Stone's interpretation of Tolstoy, the scientist is not also a blind force? Or is he still a human being with very serious preoccupations about the destiny of the species? I do not think that war today means the same thing as "war" for a gentleman who used a stone axe. And I think that the gravity of this situation should make us all aware that beyond specialization, either of military strategy or any other form of specialization, we are here concerned with the survival of the human species. We can hardly shrink from this moral responsibility we all share.

I am glad to say I belong to a part of the world known as Latin America and described, from the point of view of economics, as an underdeveloped part of the world. I say this because in Mexico recently a meeting occurred of Latin American leaders at a high political level in which the decision was taken to ban and preclude any form of atomic endeavors that might be used for destructive purposes. I am, as I say, very happy to think that underdeveloped nations may take this decision and this point of view.

I simply wish to stress the fact that I think that this is the real issue. It is certainly wonderful to know that scientists are cooperating in many fields of endeavor. But I think that the critical issue that confronts us is something more urgent than one of simply feeding the positive aspects of what, I'm sure, we are all happy about or agree with. I personally think that, in considering science, we should concentrate upon the very positive, immediate and brutal menace to our species derived from scientific progress. I am sure that in this field those present here can make much more valuable contributions than I. I should simply like to pinpoint what I think is the major area of concern.

It is far from me to pass moral judgment on Professor Anderson, his colleagues or any other man. My concern is about the future. Just as it was very complicated to design the bomb, one should not shrink because of the fact that it may be very complicated to devise international means of having some kind of guarantees that a far more destructive bomb than what was used then will not be used later.

6. Love and Human Survival

by

JOSEPH P. EVANS

I perhaps fit in somewhere between the physical scientist and the socio-
logist, because I have been raised in the discipline of the sciences, but I deal
with the stuff, as a neurological surgeon, that dreams are made of. As I
glance about me daily and see the reality of multiple races, I have often
occasion to look between the layers of skin pigment in these races. I have
not discovered significant differences in form or function beneath that
pigment. I conclude that we all are brothers. In my contact with foreign
students, over the years, I have found that the differences are only very
superficial, depending on culture and on language. Furthermore, as a
grandparent, I have children who are married to the nationals of three
different continents, North America, Latin America and Europe. I have
found that their children are no different from others I know, whether in
form, function or operations.

We are, as has been stated by Mr. Squirru, faced with a great international
hazard. As a biologist dealing with people, I am pessimistic and at the same
time optimistic. People are people; they do not subject themselves very
well to scientific analysis; and they react to their situations with very
different responses. As Mr. Nef has pointed out so poignantly in the papers
circulated prior to our meeting, the real answer to this problem is in the
realm of love.[1] Somehow science alone is not enough. The physical
sciences and the social sciences are not enough. Increasing facilities for
intercommunication are not enough.

We stand on a precipice, and without love for the human being, as a
creature worth perpetuating, I do not see any solution to our problem.

1. Cf. Nef, *The United States and Civilization*, Chicago, 1967, esp. chapter twelve; *Bridges of
Human Understanding*, New York, 1964, part III, section 8.

7. The Problem of Coexistence

by

The Honorable JAMES H. DOUGLAS

I greatly appreciate the opportunity to take part in this discussion. Professor Devons' reference to education being the province of the old, based on experience, recalls the story about the outstanding elder citizen of a midwestern town whom all respected for his unquestioned good judgment. One day he was asked to what he attributed this sound judgment and he replied, "of course, my good judgment and my wisdom are the result of experience. But the more I think about it the more I realize that most of that experience was the result of bad judgment."

In our search for world or international community I shall briefly refer to the most unfavorable aspect of our world environment; I shall mention helpful factors at work, and particularly what I believe is the most favorable political condition for the kind of coexistence that may point towards justice and peace for the peoples of the world.

In seeking to encourage the growth and spread of human understanding we find we are dealing with the interests and emotions of some three billion people now forming more than a hundred nations. Nationalism appears the strongest force in the world today. It is responsible for much in human progress. We must admit, however, that it is disruptive; it produces conflict; it separates Western nations; it separates Communist nations; it seeks to dominate; it destroys attempts to dominate; it produces irrational dangerous conflict as with India and Pakistan; it disrupts Western Europe; it proliferates new nations; it produces closed societies; but it is the basic reality of our world.

To tame this force we have achieved a world organization, the United Nations, which gives us hope for a world community of nations seeking justice and peace. It has weathered twenty-two years. It has acquired knowledge and experience. It is dealing with problems of critical importance to our future. It must be adaptable to changing conditions and flexible under the stresses and strains of forces old and new.

Perhaps the approaches to world community outside the United Nations are as important as within. They call for the breaking down of barriers to understanding, trade and friendship, between two nations or between many. This is being undertaken in a hundred ways through cooperative projects, the sharing of knowledge, joint scientific projects, travel, a broadening exchange of students, and most important, in the encourage-ment of trade. And trade has a way of breaking barriers whether or not it is encouraged to do so.

The Chairman quotes Montesquieu as writing "Wherever there is commerce there are gentle manners, and wherever there are gentle manners there is commerce." [1] My diagnosis is that commerce precedes the gentle manners, but that both are an aid to understanding and to the main-tainance of peace.

In seeking world community we are particularly concerned with ways in which the sciences, the arts, the humanities, and the social sciences can be of assistance. Where are we most likely to find effective aid in breaking down the barriers between nations? Clearly the arts and humanities provide a natural area in which common understanding should grow and flourish, but also in the physical sciences are strong forces working to break through ideological national barriers. Science abhors isolation. Here is comfort for the scientists to whom we often attribute many of our present difficulties. It is true that they have subjected all human activities to scientific exami-nation and standards, and in doing so have weakened standards that seem basic to our civilization. They have introduced technologies which have shrunk the world, and they have provided weapons which are a threat to survival. But the scientists of all countries have common interests, a common language, and generally common goals. They communicate as do businessmen in search of trade. As Professor Anderson has told us in interesting detail, they discuss nuclear power, space problems, genetics, meteorology, and they generally desire to cooperate. Only recently I became aware of our cooperation without formal agreement in the field of meteorology both with the Soviet Union and China. We can look with confidence to a constantly growing world community in science.

In the humanities and social sciences there is a different challenge to our search for community. There are not only language difficulties in that the languages are different, but the same words mean different things. Here we need creative thinking which in time might reconcile ideologies that

1. *De l'Esprit des Lois*, Paris, 1922, vol. i, p. 324. First edition 1748.

threaten expanding crusades of destruction. Here such creative historical thinking as John Nef has given, in an historical interpretation of the present that is neither Marxist nor anti-Marxist, can play an important part. Perhaps, as he suggests, the path we are on is still one of progress. Perhaps industrial civilization, trade, quantity production, peace, good manners, and interest in the welfare of other peoples, are all pointing towards world community.

When we look for the political environment in which the divisive drive of nationalism might be turned toward world community, and one that is not authoritarian, I believe we will find it is that of liberalism. And I define such liberalism in the words of my friend Professor Hayek, "liberalism which secures individual liberty under law, which recognizes that knowledge and civilization rest on tradition, and which derives from the discovery of a self-generating or spontaneous order." Such liberalism provides an order not dependent upon common purposes but upon reciprocal benefits to the participants, thus permitting a diversity of purposes subject only to rules or arrangements of respect for the rights of all participants. Professor Hayek has pointed out that the unique importance of the spontaneous order of the market is its extending the possibility of peaceful coexistence of men beyond small groups having definite common purposes, beyond tribes and beyond nations. A political environment which enables people and nations with various beliefs to seek different goals with satisfaction and mutual benefits can bring us closer to world community. The fact that the Communist world is committed against the spontaneous order does not determine that it can never coexist with the western world with benefit to itself. Coexistence can be justified by prospective and realized benefits more surely than by fear. And perhaps the realization of mutual benefits with increasing trade and communication has begun to raise the curtain of what is still the closed society of the Soviet Union.

It will be a long road through the barriers of nationalism and ideology to a community wherein men can coexist not only with mutual benefit, but with mutual confidence and respect. We will continue to search for the guideposts on that road.

PART II: THE SCIENTIFIC STUDY OF MANKIND

1. A Self-Generating Order for Society

by

F R I E D R I C H A. H A Y E K

It is very difficult to know where to begin when one would wish to comment on almost every preceding speaker. I am particularly tempted to make some remarks on the problem of the differences or similarities of the methods of the exact sciences and the social sciences which have been raised several times, and their implications for policy. But I will refrain from attacking even this problem systematically, although it has been one of my main concerns for years, and try to develop what seems to me the central point of our concern, the point which I would hardly have dared to raise if Jim Douglas had not succeeded in stating briefly, in three minutes, what I thought could not be stated in three hours. But I will make my starting point what he said, and if you think at first that what I say has no direct relevance to what has been said before, I hope you will later see that it is connected with most of the problems so far discussed.

What I want to begin with is the manner in which, from the small, tribal groups of men who were in incessant warfare with each other, some approach to an open or great society arose, in which it was at least conceivable that people should live at peace with each other. I think that the crucial difference is that the small, tribal group is what I would like to call a purpose-connected group. Professor Michael Oakeshott in London has invented for this kind of society the name of a telocratic society, a society which is kept together by the pursuit of common, particular or concrete purposes – please note, *concrete* purposes. In other words, the order of a small society presupposes that its members have particular, concrete objectives in mind, that they serve a common hierarchy of particular ends. Now, these societies which were what I would call tribal societies, relied on rules that were end-dependent, in the sense that they served the particular purposes of the group. There gradually developed from such closed societies, to which only members could belong who served the same ends, what I would call purpose-independent or open groups. The first time some member of some little savage tribe left a piece of salt at the boundary of its tribe, in the hope that a member of another tribe would find it and would leave some other gift, something new arose. People learned to collaborate with each other without pursuing the same common purpose. They both benefitted from this transaction, but they could do so without serving consciously the same ends. And gradually man learned to develop the rules which applied only to the members of the small group pursuing the same visible purposes, into rules which made peaceful coexistence possible between people who did not pursue the same common purposes. I believe it was the great achievement on the one hand of the Roman law and on the other hand of Christianity, that men developed from tribal rules, which applied only to people pursuing the same concrete ends, to universal rules which applied to all who were willing to obey the same kind of rules. You might describe this as a transition from the closed society, the society to which only those people belonged who shared and were aware of the same concrete ends, to a society where anyone belonged who merely obeyed the same abstract or general rules.

Now, there are two kinds of rules; and correspondingly two different kinds of order. A society which rests on the pursuit of common purposes, the telocratic society, is what I prefer to call an organization or an arrangement. Every activity is adjusted to the pursuit of this common hierarchy of ends by the direction of the chiefs, the headmen, or whoever commands the society. We are apt to think of organization or arrangement as the only kind of order. In fact, we are inclined to assume that wherever there is an order there must have been some arranger or designer of the order. The great achievement of the open or great society is that it produces an order spontaneously as a result of the individual's obeying abstract rules, that it is a self-generating order. Such a self-generating order is an order which, while it provides opportunities for every individual to use his own knowledge in the service of his purposes, serves as an order no particular purpose. It produces merely opportunities for everybody. That there is such a thing as spontaneous or self-generating order was the great discovery of the eighteenth century thinkers, mainly the Scottish moral philosophers; it provided the basis for much of what was first developed by biology and later by the social sciences. Indeed, the idea that a social theory has an object at all is tied up with the discovery that there is such a thing as a self-generating, spontaneous order.

This sort of theory suffers, however, from the point of view of the exact sciences, from a curious deficiency. It explains to us how an order is formed by the utilization of the knowledge possessed by thousands or millions of men, an order which, however, can never be perceived as a whole by the observing scientist. All we can do is to describe the abstract character of the order. Unlike the physical scientist, we can never insert in these formulae of the theory the detailed concrete data and proceed from a description of the abstract nature of the order to a description of its particular manifestations which we must expect.

This, I believe, means that the basis of the peaceful coexistence of men in the great society must rest on an agreement concerning rules which produce a self-generating or abstract order. We have indeed approached, in creating peaceful conditions in ever larger groups not by "organizing" them, but by the enforcement of what is called the rule of law, the general adoption and enforcement of purpose-independent rules. By purpose-independent I mean, that they do serve only the formation of an abstract order, but that they are not dependent on the pursuit of particular, concrete ends.

I think that from this very important lessons are to be learned. I think that it means that although, of course, this self-generating or abstract order is made up of many organizations which were deliberately organized, it becomes a peaceful order only because all these organizations are themselves integrated in the larger, spontaneous order, and are subject to those abstract rules which make up the larger order.

The great confusion of our times seems to me to be due to the fact that we are inclined to believe that we can achieve peace internationally by turning the world into an organization in my technical sense, instead of extending the basic principles of a spontaneous order on the international level. What we have not yet learned is what I would like to call the taming of organization. Instead of taming organizations, which are the main source of conflict today, we are led by the illusion that by creating more international organizations this will make for peace. I think that the problem of taming organizations, including the biggest one, government (which, or course, always is an organization while a society is not an organization but a spontaneous order), through subjecting them to those abstract rules of conduct which we call the rule of justice, is still the main problem ahead.

This needs one further qualification. I believe that the transition from the purpose-bound rules of the tribal or closed society to the purpose – independent formal rules of the open or great society involves a transition from rules which prescribe a particular action to rules which are essentially negative. I think we will find, if we examine the problem closely, that the great society rests on a system of rules which consist almost entirely of prohibitions, of delimitations of individual domains which prevent people from coming into conflict. We are prevented from recognizing this by several dangerous prejudices popular in our time. One of them is the idea that the positive must always be better than the negative. Now, in the field of rules needed for the great society, I am sure that the great society must rest entirely on negative rules. All positive rules presuppose a particular purpose to which people are directed, and only negative rules leave people free to pursue their own purposes within the limits necessary in order that they do not harm others.

A second and connected prejudice – and perhaps here I must disagree with John Nef – is that in this connection we ought to concentrate on the abstract rather than on the concrete. I think that the essential point of the great society is that it is an abstract order relying on abstract rules, and that we are bound only by the abstract rules that give us, as individuals, the opportunity to choose the concrete purposes.

The third point, closely connected with this, is, I am afraid, also slightly contrary to John Nef's views. I am afraid this great abstract order must be based on impersonal rules essentially of a prohibitory order, and has itself no place for love. It serves the purpose to make love possible for the individual. But love presupposes that the individual is free to choose. Love presupposes that the authority as such has nothing to do with love, because it merely delimits the spheres in which the individual can act. Love is something essentially bound to the concrete, to the particular, bound to the sphere of the individual, and ought to be kept out of all these problems of international order.

I think we will not get the international order we want, the international order of peace, by concerning ourselves with concrete particular aims, or with prescribing particular purposes. What we must aim at is what many people have vaguely called an international rule of law. Now, an international rule of law will probably not be achieved mainly by creating new international institutions. The reason why I am skeptical is that few people have yet learnt what the rule of law means – and they are rapidly forgetting it. We must remember that after all the West, and particularly the western world between the seventeenth and nineteenth century, had discovered one unique conception no other civilization had fully discovered – the conception that, if we all obey the same rules of law and concede them to other individuals, an order will result in which we are all free to pursue our own ends, but which confines government and confines coercion to the enforcement of these abstract rules.

2. The Human Sciences and the Nature of Man

by

C H A R L E S   M O R A Z É

I agree with much of what Mr. Hayek has said. I agree completely that if humanity is to avoid destruction at the hands of the new weapons, it will be the consequence of a kind of self-generating order. But the question that concerns us in a session on the so-called social sciences and the humanities is whether their study can provide us with any insights as to how such an order might be expected to evolve on the world stage.

For a long time, I believed that the study of history would provide an explanation for everything which was of concern to us. I no longer think so. History, being obviously not logical, but composed of non-recurrent events, cannot in itself be considered a science. It provides a record which is indispensable and the problem of getting this record straight is rightly a matter of concern. But predictions based on history cannot satisfy our need for certainty.

The technological revolution that mankind is presently witnessing has its origins in the physical sciences, which have endowed the potentialities for action with alarming power. Unfortunately, however, the physical sciences have come up with nothing to counterbalance a violence which they have rendered more dangerous – and which neither literature nor religion have been able to alleviate. Up to now, nothing has been able to prevent nationalism and racism from devastating Europe or from spreading throughout the world. Well-intentioned and clear-thinking men find themselves – particularly in the United States, whose industry is steeping Asia in blood – experiencing the same feeling of helplessness as those Germans who fought against Nazism or those Frenchmen who were involved in the drama of decolonization.

Throughout the world individuals, preoccupied with their daily routine, still fall easy victims to collective pride. Westerners, being the most modern, *should* be the most humble. Anthropology has taught them the relativity of all cultures; history, that every culture is indebted to other cultures. Nonetheless, they escape with difficulty the passions which the past has buried in the present.[1] The eminent anthropologist appointed by Pierre Mendes-France to govern Algeria and to settle its conflicts was unable to resist the temptation of becoming the leader of one side. Even those who fight the hardest and for the worthiest causes cannot entirely escape a certain aggressiveness, which reanimates the very aggressiveness they are fighting on the other side and which raises insurmountable obstacles to a reasoned solution. The game is lost from the start, merely because consciences (whose opposition is all the more passionate because they are similarly stirred by equally violent feelings) are not subjected to the same lucid examination.

We are fully aware that conflict is characteristic of mankind and that greater power has not made men better. Nonetheless, we are not entirely helpless in the face of these paroxysms of disorder which today's technology has made so dangerous. It has been said for many centuries, and without ever being entirely disproven, that moral strength is a variable of knowledge. This supposition makes hope possible, with a concomitant need to know and make known the nature of man, and the origins and rightful limits of his ambition.

If moral behavior is a variable of knowledge, the knowledge must be simple enough to be shared, and sufficiently definite and permanent to create the kind of consensus which different cultures have derived from the great religions which held them together. In terms of a more modern, but also universal and positivist outlook, the most successful consensus to date has been derived from Marx. His doctrine is obviously not perfect: it did not succeed in pushing into action the proletariat to which it was addressed. But before questioning Marxism's validity, we would do well to consider whether there are not some very good reasons why millions of people adopted, and continue to adopt it. The point is not so much the materialism of Marx: there are many who think themselves idealists who are in fact just as materialist. Marxism's real value was to have given back belief to peoples in despair. One cannot improve on Marx without acknowledging his success and without realizing also that men as they are today have never been more in need of something with the dimensions and ambitiousness of Marx's achievement; that is, a statement concerning what

---

1. J. de Bourbon Busset, "Seeing Ourselves as Others See Us", *Bridges of Human Understanding*, Nef ed., New York, 1964, pp. 16–17.

moves them, what are their origins, their present situation and their possible goals.

If I suggest, for moral reasons, Marxism as a possibly incomplete and provisional, but nonetheless effective model for those who have chosen to study some aspect of human nature, it is not by sheer love of paradox. Until men go beyond the limits of their particular disciplines and combine to work out critiques and continuously to reconstruct a larger synthesis, they will not serve science and learning, which might thus attain their highest fulfilment. They will serve rather the technocracy of the physicists. It is not presumptuous, therefore, to hope that, before the century ends, the social sciences will have proven the validity of a general hypothesis, an effective guide for the advance of our space-age civilization. This goal must be reached before cataclysmic events succeed in destroying everything.

It is necessary to point out that the social sciences, systematically organized around a central influx governed by the unity of man, will not cause the sources of faith, action and literature to dry up. They will merely provide humans with a few points of certainty at a moment when mankind possesses too many frightening weapons to allow itself the luxury of going continuously astray. But if this large-scale synthesis is necessary, the fact that it must be based on the behavioral sciences – that is, on precisely those disciplines which are the least certain and the least systematically coordinated among themselves – makes its achievement singularly difficult.

There is no one basic knowledge from which all other knowledge can be derived. However, it is by seeking the relationship between the different branches that knowledge progresses, and it is in this task that the sciences and education can come together. The necessary precondition for the unity of mankind is what scholars decide among themselves on the nature of man, both present and future.

Thus, scholars must unite to discuss matters of concern to their own disciplines; they must, in addition, devote an increasing portion of their time and effort to clarifying as much as possible developments, both within their particular sector and within themselves, in relation to the past by which they were formed and taught, while at the same time confining the discussion to matters which can be objects of experience. They will then be concerned with the manner in which their intellectual work is carried out, an action which can be helped or hindered by their emotions, whether by excessive exhilaration or excessive depression. They will become conscious of the needs and functions of the human body, which constitutes the only positive reality genuinely common to all men.

Then, perhaps, the misfortunes of other men and other cultures will cease to be treated as abstractions. Everything in literature and the arts which restores men to a state of sensitivity and sensuality will help and induce the technologists, the economists and the politicians to render due respect to the importance, the demands and reactions, the susceptibility and fragility, of that basic capital entrusted to man which is life itself.

3. Interventions on behalf of the Arts and the Physical Sciences

(A) THE ARTS

by

Rafael Squirru

I was struck by some of the remarks made by Professor Morazé and I feel very reluctant, really, to take issue with such an intelligent paper. But, after all, there are other kinds of conscience as well, and I would not feel that I were really doing what I should if I did not.

If I understood him aright, and also in the light of our earlier discussion of the experimental sciences, I take it he is suggesting that the human sciences and therefore history have more and more to adapt themselves to the exact sciences in order to win the prestige that will bring in the dollars, to begin with! In this respect I know how serious is this preoccupation of Professor Morazé, because I direct a department of culture, which is to some extent a department of human sciences. In the budget of our organization we are confronted with the fact that since, of course, the economists have invented the science of priorities, they inevitably have decided that the prior needs of man belong in the field of economics and other somewhat more exact sciences within the social sphere, and that subjects such as history or philosophy, poetry or the arts are of secondary importance.

This is not just a joke I am making. It is a fact which confronts us when the moment arrives to distribute the means to carry out our programs.

But is this justification enough for us humanists to don the disguise of the more respectable gentlemen who deal with the exact sciences? I, for one, take issue with such a disguise. I think it is our increasing responsibility to maintain the role that up till now has been ours. We are custodians of the mystery of man. You cannot reduce this mystery to any form of exact measurement. I regard exact measurement in connection with non-scientific subjects as a form of heresy which has grown with the scientific thinking of the last century. This is a real menace, it seems to me, to the kind of testimony that is properly ours as humanists to give. The temptations to yield are great. I think we have to resist them, even at the price of appearing to some unimaginative persons as, at best, less reputable investigators, or, at worst, quacks!

You may now ask me, well, what is this mystery that you are trying to keep in custody? That brings us into a new realm of thought that we explore in later parts of these discussions.[1]

(B) THE PHYSICAL SCIENCES

by

SAMUEL DEVONS

I am prompted to re-enter the discussion because of the different courses taken by the last two participants. It may seem from what they have told us that the issue is between imitating science or repudiating science: either the social sciences may imitate or approximate the natural sciences, or else in some sense defy them.

I do not think the choice lies between these alternatives. This rather strong attitude toward the natural sciences comes from a misconception. The misconception derives from a sort of passion that people feel towards solving problems, towards prediction and control. They believe that this is the primary or exclusive function of the natural sciences. Now, if one examines the natural sciences in all their parts, I do not think one gets this impression at all.

The remark has been made here, in several different contexts, that the natural sciences are successful in making predictions. We all know that. Natural science, in its ability to predict, in its ability to control, has had a large measure of success. This is often demonstrated by the material products that ensue from its intellectual activities.

However, one must not overlook the fact that, within science itself, what is predicted relates, essentially, not to the present but to the past problems of science. One can take an intelligent young boy or girl of sixteen today, and in the course of a few months explain to that boy or girl essentially all the problems that confronted Newton, the genius of his time. But they are not the problems that confront science or scientists today.

The point I am leading to is this: Science does not only solve problems; it

1. See below, esp. Parts III and IV.

creates problems, within science and without science, and the very activity of solving one problem poses for science a new problem.

I hope I shall not be accused of immodesty if I take physics as a pattern. It is normally so chosen, as a pattern *par excellence*, of the exact sciences. Therefore one imagines that it reaches a sort of perfection of explanation. This is very far from the truth.

One may ask, at what stage in the physical sciences was the proximity between understanding and the phenomena to be explained closest. I do not think the answer would be, the present day. Some people might put it at 1700, some at 1900. But not the present day, because the power of physics, and the technology it creates, have presented it with far more problems, perhaps far deeper problems, than the ones it has solved. And this will continue to be so.

I think a strong lesson could be learned here about these developments in the physical sciences and the question of imitation by social sciences. Can sociology imitate physics? Sociology is not concerned primarily with past problems. It is concerned with present and future problems. If one compares, for example, the science of anthropology with sociology, one sees this quite clearly. One can explain things in the past, from a large perspective of a thousand years or ten thousand miles, much more easily than the things that are at hand.

It is no different in the natural sciences, except that one is overwhelmed in the natural sciences by the material success into believing that the logic of their development, their intellectual development, is something different. But it is not really different. In social science there is not the same material success – there is not the same yardstick. One wants success in prediction, which natural science has not given us in that sense, at all.

I think a good example, one which has been dwelt on, is Marxism. Possibly it "solved a problem." But whether it did or did not is hardly the issue, because the problem is clearly now one of the past, not of the present or the future.

From the time the problem was solved the problem became irrelevant. This is characteristic of sociology and it is also in some degree characteristic of physics. The matters that are solved are not the current problems of science.

Another comparison is sometimes made between biology and sociology. Insofar as their subject matter is concerned they look superficially very close, much closer than the physical sciences and sociology. Yet to draw an analogy between them can be very dangerous. Here I will take advantage, if I may, of Mr. Douglas' very apt story concerning experience and judgment. In biology evolution occurs as a result of mistakes, of essentially fatal mistakes. So there is one major distinction between biological evolution and human social evolution. In human evolution one rules out, a priori, such a solution. For the human species, the fatal mistake is no solution at all.

PART III: THE CLASSICS AS EDUCATION

1. Two Pre-Modern Muslim Historians: Pitfalls and Opportunities in Presenting them to Moderns

by

MARSHALL G. S. HODGSON

We know that commitment to truth is a moral act, and generally that intellectual life depends on moral qualities, but it is hard to do much about this fact and we often neglect it in practice. But it is of peculiar importance in my field,[1] and here I propose to remind us of it and of some of its implications.

A scholar studying pre-Modern civilizations has the responsibility of discovering and effectively presenting to Modern human beings the meaning for us of heritages from ages so strikingly different from our own that it is hard to persuade ordinary people that they can have any intrinsic significance for us. Pre-Modern culture is alien not merely because it presupposes differing local assumptions and expectations, such as differ among Modern peoples, but because it does not share in the far-reaching set of mind and of life that came with the transformations of the seventeenth and eighteenth centuries. Despite our eager admiration for a few of the top classics of art or letters, and despite a pervasive seminal influence, the culture from before those centuries does not enter much, directly, into the workaday world of Modern culture, except in certain privileged spheres like some aspects of religion. Not everyone, like some physicists, feels he need know nothing that was done in his field earlier than a few decades ago; nor does everyone, like some artists, see all past traditions as no more than a storehouse of suggestions for incidental elements of design, no tradition having any claims on his loyalty. Yet with all my devotion to the classical, I find it necessary to point out to the rare student who has had Latin in school but no French or German that, though Latin was a great language, in my field there are no monographs written in it usable for

1. Hodgson was primarily concerned with the history of Islamic civilization in relation to world history.

term-papers or for theses. For in fact there is a remarkably great gulf set between our age, for which multiple large-scale technical specialization sets the pace in almost every sphere of life, and any earlier age. Time and again the historian of pre-Modern times is struck with how much even the most distant of pre-Modern citied societies had in common, as to basic presuppositions, in contrast to Modern society. And, as a corollary, it is increasingly true that all Modern societies have more in common with each other (especially on the decisive levels of historical action) than has any of them with its own pre-Modern antecedents.

Accordingly, both the pitfalls and the opportunities that await a scholar trying to present the pre-Modern Islamicate heritage to Modern Westerners lie far more in the difference between pre-Modern and Modern than in that between Islamicate and Western. I have found, for instance, that in my course on the Qur' ân, just the same points need to be brought out so as to make it come alive, whether the student is of Muslim background or of Western. (I must except the more dedicated products of Muslim religious schools, whose reactions are strikingly parallel to those of their opposite numbers among the Catholics.) At moments, one could suppose that the essential problems in presenting a pre-Modern work to Modern college graduates were the same, whatever the cultural affiliation of either the pre-Modern work or the Modern students. But this is not quite so. The differences among the heirs to the several traditions still dig deep. An avowedly atheistic "Muslim" student in my Qur' ân course did indeed respond to the same sorts of elucidations that the Western students responded to; but the outcome was in one case, at least, different: the ex-Muslim student did not merely appreciate the Qur' ân as a great work, as did the others, but began turning to it for practical daily spiritual inspiration. Teaching a Western classic to non-Westerners, or an Islamicate classic to non-Muslims, still presents special problems of reaching across modern cultural gaps, superadded to the problems presented by the gap between pre-Modern and Modern.

This is especially so in the field of religious tradition, which still has at least its indirect effects even among those sectors of a population that are most consciously emancipated from any religious allegiance (witness the most lively strains in recent Soviet Russian literature, where the Christian tradition, mediated through Tolstoy or Dostoievski, can color imagery and ideals deeply). But I am not going to pick a religious document for my present remarks, for that would be bound to raise special problems. I shall pick instead two historical documents from the pre-Modern Islamicate tradition: the work of two historians (who had little more in common than that they were both products of Islamicate culture). The work of a historian can have its own greatness – which, since it consists in interpretation of great human events, is in some ways peculiarly accessible, not only to another historian, but to anyone who thinks about human events. Even so, I shall not pick the one Islamicate historian that some modern Westerners have heard of, Ibn-Khaldûn; partly because those who have heard of him probably suffer from misconceptions of his work that I'd rather not have to clear away.

Ibn-Jarir al-Tabari (d. 923) dealt with the early history of the Muslims. One of the central problems he was confronted with was how the Islamic vision was to be realized in actual social life after the death of the Prophet. Muhammad had been a consummate visionary, general, diplomat, and leader of men: he had created a powerful social-religious community, which had soon found itself in a position to seize power over the lands from Nile to Oxus from the hands of the Sasanian agrarian gentry. There seemed to be no problem in the Muslim community's maintaining power (in fact, most members of the old agrarian gentry proceeded to join the Muslim community). But Muhammad's work had meant not only creation of a powerful community, but charging that community with a dynamic vision of social ideals. It was the ideals that seemed, in the early generations of Islam, to be more potential than actual; and for a growing minority of concerned Muslims, the great problem of history was how to realize those ideals within the social framework provided by the community's power. Tabari's history traces, in effect, the dilemmas so produced within the community. Tabari represented a group of Muslims who believed that the answer did not lie in military revolt in the vain hope of raising to power an ideal ruler (many concerned Muslims tried this again and again); rather, the community should be held together even if this required acceptance of the current rulers; but then the moral inadequacy of those rulers must be recognized and counteracted. The answer lay in developing among the body of the Muslims themselves the kind of clarity and unity on legal standards of the good life that no ruling dynasty could ignore; if the concerned Muslims could establish a law that all would acknowledge, it would become less important who was ruler, for the area within which he could act arbitrarily would be so reduced as to be socially unimportant. In fact – and partly thanks to Tabari's own efforts, both as historian and as legist – to some degree these Muslims succeeded; though only in part.

Tabari's history, then, focussed on the fate of the Muslim community as carrier of the Islamic ideals, and in particular on the personal decisions of individuals who bore particular responsibility for that fate in the successive choices that faced the community – setting down how well or how poorly they fulfilled their responsibility. But this trait is not directly visible. For his method is rather indirect. He wrote, in fact, few sentences of his own, and absolutely no judgments on his subjects. Rather, he strung together anecdotal reports of the events, carefully documenting each report by listing the series of witnesses through whom it had come to him – in such a form as "x told me that y said to him that z reported having seen . . ." (The same form was relevant whether he had collected an oral report passed down in some family's lore – "x told me from his ancestors" – or was listing those who had passed a written text on from one generation of students to the next, ensuring the correct reading despite the imperfection of manuscripts before printing.) But the reports were neither chosen nor placed at random. To his students, he pointedly explained that though his history seemed inordinately long (it fills many volumes), he had selected only a tenth of the material that had come to his attention. The consequences of his arrangement of the selected anecdotes were almost as important.

The method can be illustrated in his discussion of the killing of 'Uthman, the third successor of Muhammad, by Muslim mutineers. At first sight, the narrative seems repetitious and somewhat chaotic, for each anecdote is reported whole just as it was told, and 'Uthman's death is mentioned many times – as the ultimate consequence of some preliminary event – before it is described for itself. But eventually we see that there emerge two main sets of anecdotes. Much of set A is reported from one man, al-Waqidi, an earlier gatherer of such reports, who had a not altogether favorable reputation for accuracy among those who studied the many men through whom these historical reports were transmitted. In this set of anecdotes, al-Waqidi's reports are interspersed with reports from various other sources, some of which complement or confirm al-Waqidi, and some of which – by the very circumstances of their telling (fully retained, as we have seen, in their presentation as independent units) – criticize him in detail. The anecdotes are mostly quite humanly credible in themselves, and present a realistically ambiguous picture of the moral responsibility of the various parties in what was a rather complex affair. As to set B, all of it is reported from one man, Sayf b. 'Umar, who had a very poor reputation as a transmitter of reports, but into whose reports Tabari introduces neither corroborative nor corrective anecdotes whatever. Sayf's anecdotes, like those in set A, are fairly lively, but many of them seem staged or are humanly quite incredible; and the whole story unambiguously aligns the "good guys", who defended 'Uthman, against the "bad guys" who fought him.

The section as a whole begins and ends with set A; but just as the anecdotes of that set have built up to a point of climax – 'Uthman's door has been beaten down and he is about to be killed – set B is introduced, telling most of the story all over again with its monolithic and sometimes stagy tone; only when it is completed do we go back to set A to finish the story. For readers who want a clear, straightforward narrative – and are not put off by Sayf's bad reputation – the choice between the two pictures is obvious: they will take set B, Sayf's story. But for readers who have a sense of the human and of the dramatic, Sayf appears as an unwelcome interruption – all the more obviously so, for being placed as a solid indigestible bloc right at the height of tension; he serves only to point up the ambiguities of the account in set A.

But to see more fully what Tabari has done here, we must note the implications of the two sets of reports for his primary historical concerns. From the point of view of the Sunni Muslims with whom Tabari was affiliated, it was necessary to show that all the associates of Muhammad had been sound in religious essentials, whatever their disputes among themselves; for this assertion had come to be identified with their special conception of Muslim solidarity. Sayf's story (set B) did this in a simplistic way: all Muhammad's associates were good guys, and 'Uthman's friends. For those who did not want to think further, it was as irenic a description of what happened as could be looked for. But set A of the anecdotes suggested that many of the most prominent associates of Muhammad had been in fact opposed to 'Uthman and did nothing to prevent his murder. Such an approach might be upsetting to a good Sunni Muslim; but set A was not left at that. The first and last anecdotes in the set stand apart from the chronological sequence and suggest, with the help of other anecdotes in the set, that the fault lay in basic dilemmas of power, which evoked honest differences of opinion; and they even hint at something of Tabari's own solutions. The reader, then, can (if he is so inclined) read the passages as an apologia for the subsequent Sunni position on the nature of the Muslim community. But the perceptive reader will be forced to consider the alternative presented, which is equally orthodox, but on a totally different level, and which will force him to see the far-reaching problem of power which lay at the heart of the Muslim dilemma; and so to appreciate more fully the meaning of the effort of the Muslim legists to create a law that can by-pass the holders of power. On all points of explicit doctrine, Tabari normally went along with prevailing Muslim sentiment in Baghdad at the time; yet he was nearly lynched by the ultra-orthodox mob; and we can guess why.

Sometimes we believe that, with the institutions of representative and constitutional democracy, we have long since solved the particular problem of power with which Tabari was wrestling. I am not so confident that the problem is so safely solved even in our terms. But in any case, Tabari's problem was not simply how to control power; it was how to control power *for the sake of a dynamic idealism*. Perhaps thoughtful Communists might be in a better position to recognize the full extent of the problem than those of us who feel rather self-satisfied with our society. But if we take seriously the whole vision with which Tabari was inspired, we may find that, for us, a more interesting form of the problem – to which Tabari may still prove relevant – might be: how to embody a transcendent social vision in life where the structure of power seems tied to a received social balance which seems to exclude any revolutionary idealism.

The second historian I shall discuss lived six hundred years after Tabari. Tabari wrote in Baghdad, capital of the powerful Muslim Caliphate when Muslims still formed a single social body and Arabic was still their common language of culture (though not the native tongue of most Muslims – Tabari himself, for instance, was an Iranian), and the cultural and political impulses that issued from Muhammad's work were still recognizably in continuity with his original labors. Six hundred years later, Abulfazl 'Allami (d. 1602) lived at Agrah in northern India under the great Timuri (or "Mughal") Muslim empire. In many ways the continuity of cultural tradition was unbroken from Tabari's time; but the Caliphate had long since disappeared and the great monarchs of Islamdom (and in particular the Ottomans in the Mediterranean, the Safavids of Iran, and the Timurids of India) all traced their political origin to later Turkic power; and among them all, the prime language of culture was Persian. The unity of the Muslims had evolved into a subtle international network of legal and social relations, extending from Morocco and Senegal to Java, and from Zanzibar to Kazan and northern Siberia. The Islamicate tradition was richly cosmopolitan and sophisticated.

What inspited Abulfazl as a historian was the civilizational opportunity presented by Timuri agrarian absolutism in wealthy, industrious India. No dynastic family has ever, probably, presented so consistently high a level of personal taste, in the arts and even the sciences, over so long a period as the Timurids, who raised what was already becoming a tradition of high patronage of the arts into a family responsibility to the world. Probably the

greatest of these Timurid rulers was Akbar (d. 1605), whose personal
patronage of painting, of architecture, and of scholarship seems to have
had decisive effects in developing the magnificent cultural life of Muslim
India in the later sixteenth and seventeenth centuries (among us, the most
famous monument of the period is the Taj Mahall).

Abulfazl's problem was how to persuade the privileged classes to recognize the possibilities for civilization that an increasingly centralized
agrarian power, combined with far-flung mercantile cosmopolitanism, had
produced among them: the possibilities for general cultivation of all
human potentialities, in the arts especially but in all departments of life,
under the auspices of the spiritual principle of *sulh-e kull*, "universal conciliation", or "universal peace"; or at least, how to persuade them not to
sabotage the high civilization that did seem about to bud forth among
them and to be bringing a general humanistic peace. They must be kept
from falling back into the communalism and obscurantism of the several
rival religious and even cultural traditions, which would ruin these hopes –
most notably the communalism of Muslims against Hindus, but generally
any pettiness of vision that would limit the horizons, which for Abulfazl
were as open to Europe and China, when these had anything good to offer,
as to the Arabic or Persian or Indic traditions. Abulfazl's work was widely
read in subsequent generations and probably did have some of the intended
effect.

Abulfazl's historical method was to present the Timurid dynasty as an
ideal dynasty and Akbar as an ideal monarch and even as an ideal man;
presenting him as a patron of civilization and as exemplar in his own
person of the personality traits that required to be cultivated in individuals
if civilization was fully to develop. This was not simply an exercise in
edifying fiction, painting the ideal and then trying to give it prestige by
assigning it a famous name. (For one thing, Akbar was still alive when he
wrote, and the reader could compare the original.) In fact, Akbar actually
was one of the greatest royal patrons the arts have known (it has been
seriously suggested that it was his personal intervention in spotting and
singling out certain obscure Indian-bred painters, even while still patron-
izing their famous Iranian masters, that launched the Indo-Timuri or
"Mughal" style of painting on its brilliant career); he took a restless and
often productive interest in everything from breeding better fruit trees and
new mechanical inventions to calendar reform and the naming of fashion-
able clothing; and most particularly, he listened to so many disputations
about religion that finally he undertook to guide disciples himself, in the
manner of a Muslim mystical master, on a spiritual path peculiarly adapted

to the busy, cosmopolitan life of the court. (This last was not a mere expression of vanity: those few who became disciples of the royal confessor received no preference at all when it came to worldly promotions.)

But Abulfazl's history was also not simply a chronicling of Akbar's amazing personality. He was tireless, indeed, in tracking down factual details about military events or fiscal administration or court etiquette and even the price of various foods purchased for the royal kitchens. But his work was carefully organized to mirror, even in its symbolism, his vision of the role of the perfected man among men, and of men in the natural world. The principle of *sulh-e kull*, which he makes much of, is not merely a principle of political conciliation; it defines a particular stage of the soul's inward progress, which expresses itself on the level of civilized ability to assimilate the best cultural achievement of all peoples, as well as to work out a modus vivendi with all rivals or potential enemies, but which is pointless if it is not a part of a dynamic inward growth of the soul toward the next stage, "mahabbat-e kull", "universal love", and then on to the full Sufi mystical God-realization. His picture of the life of the court moves outward from Akbar till it finally encompasses the life of humble peasants and the most distant provinces; but it does so not simply in reflection of courtly propriety, but by way of showing how the truly civilized man will at once learn to enjoy, and labor to foster, all the rich diversity that nature and human society have combined to make available to him.

Now here we have two great works of historical writing which the humanist must try to make accessible to Modern human beings: partly for what the Modern may learn from them in the way of experience, suggestion, or general edification; perhaps more, for what they tell us of the hopes and fears of our fellow human beings of another age, which must be, in some degree, a measure of our own hopes and fears, of their pettiness or their soundness and perspective. Possibly neither writer was so great a historian as the more famous Ibn-Khaldûn, and I am willing to concede that Tabari was a greater man than Abulfazl, but they were both great figures.

The most important difficulties in interpreting these historians to Moderns stem not from their belonging to a regional civilization foreign to the majority of Moderns, but from the very fact that they are pre-Modern. Differences simply in ethnic setting – differences of language and, more important, all the cultural assumptions that go with language – seem to yield fairly readily before the sensitive translator and the skillful annotator. To be sure, we are far from a satisfactory solution of all such difficulties; but – except in certain respects that we shall go into further on – they are essentially technical; in principle, another generation or two of scholars ought to surmount them even for the most remote of the better-documented cultures. But with differences of basic outlook between pre-Modern and Modern, the problem is greater. I shall single out three points where that is involved.

In almost any pre-Modern culture, the genre form of any work, whether of art or of letters, was very precisely defined, and the rules of the genre moulded the individual work far more unswervingly than has been the case in Modern works, even before the recent rebellion against all lines of genre form. And especially in the case of the non-Western classics, the genres were often strikingly different from the Modern (which, even among non-Westerners, often show a certain affiliation to various pre-Modern Occidental genres). Tabari's "history" is like nothing the West has seen, or modern Islamdom either: its narrative takes the technical form of what are called *hadith* reports, its documentation takes the technical form of what are called *isnads*, and if one does not see the rationale of the form, one is bound to miss the point: Tabari comes to appear both repetitious and credulous, where acquaintance with the form would indicate he was graphic and critical. Abulfazl's "history" is in the form of a eulogy and he was very conscious of what this required. Indeed, he points it out on occasion to the reader in so many words – but unfortunately only at abnormal cruxes; if the reader does not share the basic notion he has of the form, even the times when he makes an explicit reference to it will be lost on the reader. If one does not recognize a eulogy as a respectable genre, as it was in the Persian tradition, one will see obsequious exaggeration where he who knows and discounts the form sees unusual moderation and unusual fidelity to actuality.

Closely related to the difference of genre is a difference in what was expected to be public and what private. In all pre-Modern societies, a considerable portion of the intellectual life (and even sometimes other aspects of culture) was esoteric: for instance, chemical experiment might go very far, but we find it hard to get at from the old texts, because it was almost universally regarded as an esoteric field which was to be disguised from the general public. In no other society was the esoteric so prevalent, however, as the Islamicate. Practically all really interesting Islamicate writers disguised their thought to some degree. Abulfazl did this systematically (as did Ibn-Khaldûn) on the basis of an acknowledged doctrine, which every sophisticated reader knew, that the surest way to avoid leading astray half-prepared readers for whom a little learning might be a dangerous thing was to compose a work in such a way that only the perceptive would be astute enough to get its true drift. Tabari did not yet own any such doctrine, so far as I know, but he did at least (at special points) provide alternative readings for the ordinary mind and for the perspicuous one. This esotericism makes for obvious problems in interpretation, including the danger of reading into a text more than is there (for the author explicitly requires that one read into it at least something of his latent intention). But it raises perhaps still more urgently a moral question: what the author chose to conceal, we may not always have the right to disclose by full explication – even assuming we are competent to be sure we understand in the first place. Yet our Modern ethos, at least in relatively free countries, is not geared to an esoteric approach; hence without such explication, even the most perspicuous are likely to miss the point altogether.

Both the above points reflect functional differences between the situation of the pre-Modern individual and the Modern. We have a different sense of the pace of historical change, for the Modern individual can be a historical initiator in a sense that was generally inaccessible to the pre-Modern (hence, in large measure, the new attitude to genre form, for instance, which is part of a more radical attitude to creativity and innovation generally). We have a different sense of our relation to our environment, being debarred by technical and institutional complexities from full overall intellectual control of what we deal with, except at a very abstract level (and hence, among serious persons, the esoteric has become an irrelevant category – none can understand a special subject anyway save by participation in a specialized public discipline; the esoteric has been replaced by the lore of the specialist, even more closely guarded than the esoteric ever could be). Finally, we have a different sense of the intellectual possibilities open to us; we can, on the one hand, assume so massive a division of intellectual labor among us that for the first time we can count on having precise control of a massive amount of "fact"; yet, on the other hand, since we cannot, any one of us, control all the "known" facts that are relevant to any given major question, we can hardly hope to express any total vision of life with the assurance that many a pre-Modern could gain. Compared to these points, I would suppose that our unprecedented global outlook and even our evolutionary outlook are almost secondary.

In the histories we are discussing, it is a different sense of facts on the one hand and of total vision on the other that imposes the greatest obstacle to our understanding. For our two historians, accuracy as to "fact" was much less important than validity as to life-vision, in part because it seemed much less accessible. Neither supposed that the main purpose of a historian was to get at raw "facts" and then interpret them one by one. Tabari explicitly doubted how close he could get to certain kinds of facts, though indeed he did his best; but he was concerned with putting such reports as were available, about an overall sequence of events which everyone would know about, into as constructive as possible a light. His intention was to build a godly society, and he knew just what that would be. To be sure, he was sufficiently reliable in this selecting of data (and his documenting of it) for his work to have become the indispensable foundation of all Modern studies into the "facts" of the period. Abulfazl, likewise, has latterly been used chiefly as a mine of data because he was so exact; he is just for Indo-Timuri history what Tabari is for early Muslim history. Yet he also was not specially concerned with facts on an ultimate level, however much pains he took to get them: he quite unashamedly states plain falsities, even uses them for major debating points, provided he can assume the audience will know they are falsities. For his interest was in a philosophical analysis of human civilization, and he inherited something of the moralistic attitude to the anecdote displayed by the Sufi mystics, whose world-view he was adapting to a life out in society. And I must add that even the great Ibn-Khaldûn, often seen as a model of "modernity" in his critical sociological outlook, may deliberately present an account that cannot be accurate, just because it brings out certain philosophical juxtapositions which he regards as relevant.

These points of difference between Modern and pre-Modern are not to be sloughed aside, even if that could be done without eviscerating the great work being studied. For surely an important part of the value of these works for us is precisely that they reflect a constellation of human life that we can hardly duplicate now, and thereby throw a special perspective on our own Modern situation. But we will find that the difficulties they produce are far less easily overcome than the more technical difficulties resulting from simple ethnic differences. The difficulties are essentially of a moral order: we find it hard to accept the moral perspective in which the pre-Modern works can truly bear fruit for us. We find it difficult to tolerate, even on a provisional basis, the seeming traditionalism and artificiality of a fixed genre, the seeming snobbishness of an esoteric guise, and most especially so contrary an evaluation of facts and of vision.

The moral difficulties are only accentuated by such differences as are still significant among Moderns of different cultural heritages. The difference between the Modern Westerner and the Modern Muslim, when it comes to the great Occidental and Islamicate classics, is partly a matter of a margin of familiarity with certain elements in the heritage and with a few of the classics themselves. The Muslims, indeed, are still closer in certain ways, even when trained in a modern university, to their pre-Modern heritage than are their opposite numbers in the West. Moreover, especially in art and in letters and most especially in religion, there persists a sense of style that derives from the pre-Modern classics even when they are little read or viewed. (A yet wider "formative" influence is real; but, I think, it is often overrated as to its direct effect on the intelligibility of the classics.)

But in my limited experience I have come to suspect that even more important is a potent residual sense of loyalty, which predisposes people to see significance or the reverse in the materials they approach. Among Muslims, because of their peculiar relation to the process of Modernity since the end of the eighteenth century, this is fairly explicit: sometimes the Western classics are approached even overtly with mistrust as one might approach a powerful and insidious enemy; more often, I suppose, this mistrust remains unconscious. Among Westerners, this relationship is more disguised by the seeming objectivity we can more readily afford; yet this "objectivity" has often expressed a smug sense of superiority, dating from the same eighteenth century and growing out of the same events. Careful studies have shown the degree to which even leading Islamicists have been determined, in their approach to the products of Islamicate culture, by their several Western allegiances, religious or cultural. It seems to be very hard for even an open-minded Westerner to escape the presumption that he is dealing with an exotic curiosity, and to approach an Islamicate work with the openness of expectation that can open up its treasures for him.

When the reader does not succeed in overcoming the difficulties that prevent his genuinely appreciating a pre-Modern work, he tends to fall into certain unavoidable and even rather attractive pitfalls. These pitfalls themselves reflect the same Modern temper that prevented a more positive appreciation: for they express the darker side of that massive technical specialization on which the achievements of Modern civilization have been built. I shall sum them up under two headings, reductivism and modernism; both of which have their effects at every level, from sheer translating on up.

Reductivism is the habit of mind of those historians who occupy themselves, indeed, with a great piece of work, but who treat it as merely the sum of ingredients that are not great. Great historic deeds can be so handled, or philosophies, or works of art – where everything is precisely dated and measured, and "influences" and techniques are probed and proven, but nothing is said about what was actually done: what problems were being solved, what it was their solution made possible – and what further artistic dilemmas the solution produced, to be resolved in the next monument. By such omissions all the serious questions are escaped, and yet one can appear elaborately learned and scientifically critical. Indeed, as we know, it can appear to be a virtue to avoid the real questions: for it is undeniable that all such secondary questions must indeed be solved if obvious errors in handling a given work are to be avoided; and the solving of such questions requires the intensive work that comes with specialization, and can use up the full time even of the specialist. Attention paid to questions of intent or of outcome comes to appear subjective, capricious and at best premature.

I am afraid that we see such tendencies at their very worst in my particular field, Islamic studies, though even here there are honorable exceptions. Such a habit of mind can turn our two historians into mere mines for facts or, at most, mere "examples" of their respective genres. Tabari has served the philologian well. In the philological specialist's attempt to get at the history of words – often more precisely ascertainable than the history of facts – Tabari's careful documentation has allowed him to date usages with rewarding precision; and Tabari has served as a monumental example of the use of the method of hadîth reports and isnâd documentation, illustrating the possibilities and defects of that exotic method (which, of course, the Modern philologian would never dream of using himself). And it is always complained that Tabari is badly organized. But no-one seems to have studied even what he was doing with the hadîth method – or how what he did with it affected the hadîth method itself – which was, in fact, never the same after him. The archive historians have done something comparable with Abulfazl, whose abundant statistics have been pored over endlessly for establishing the details of sixteenth-century administration and economic life. As to translation of these great historians for a wider public than those who read Persian or Arabic, the same spirit has prevailed. Abulfazl is so translated that what is distinctive about his philosophical system falls away either into casual rhetoric or into more or less approximate Western equivalents, which no longer mesh together as in the original; what matters is rather his tax lists. Tabari has not been translated at all – the philologian is concerned, after all, only with the words in their Arabic form; except for one late section, which is hardly representative of Tabari's primary concerns but happens to include a rather romantic and also rather savage episode nicely illustrative of exotic degeneracy.

This brings us already to the other side of the consequences of specialism; that is, modernism: when a work has been made manageable by being reduced to its ingredients, then the scholar, at least vaguely aware, still, that he has taken responsibility for an important piece of the human heritage, may feel the need to reconstitute it into something resembling an integral work of the mind. The nearest temptation is to make of a writer just another Modern man, to be appreciated for his approximation to Modern insights. In translating, this can lead to highly impressionistic effects, and Ibn-Khaldûn has especially suffered in this respect: the English translation is so drastically misleading as to be unusable. The problem is, in part, that some philologians and archive historians are so unused to taking a broader view, that when they try to make something accessible to an ordinary person, they do not do so by digging deeper, following out the basic questions involved – which ramify into fields where they are not trained (e.g., sociology, ecology, psychology of religion, philosophy, economics, etc.); rather, they do so by sticking yet more closely to the surface. (The specialist probably could not do this, did not his own sense of pride in his specialism lead him to see the general reader with more condescension than respect.) This can mean looking for something in the writer that seems familiar on the only level that some specialists can be sure the "ordinary" reader will be acquainted with – or that they may be acquainted with themselves, beyond their specialty: the level of popular fad. Ibn-Khaldûn is often seen as anticipating nineteenth-century sociology (which is not just a fad, of course, except when so used). And Abulfazl is analyzed as "tolerant" of Hindus and his work is judged, with some presumption, on the basis of how close it comes to an adequate modern notion of "toleration". But this notion of toleration is only marginally relevant to the Indo-Timuri social situation, and to Abulfazl's purposes in particular – for him "sulh-e kull" is not general toleration in a legal sense, but a spiritual principle of which a particular sort of toleration, a toleration far, however, from any spirit of levelling, was a by-product,

It will already be becoming apparent, what is required in our quest to make the pre-Modern masterpieces meaningful to Moderns. To transcend the presuppositions about the very nature of creativity that Modernity imposes on us, to escape the subtle influences of loyalty to our particular heritage, even to overcome the dilemmas and pitfalls of specialism, requires more than merely academic warnings and a policy of wide reading on the part of specialists. We need certain qualities of soul. Perhaps we can pinpoint these with the help of Mollâ Sadrà, an Iranian philosopher of the early seventeenth century. He said that every philosopher – and by that, he meant every inquirer, scientist or scholar – must have four traits: he must be able to renounce wealth (read, I suppose, government contracts); be able to renounce status (read, perhaps, the status of doing without government contracts); be able to renounce conformism; and be able to renounce rebelliousness.

We have come to realize better than we once did, I suppose, how important the first two sorts of detachment can be; especially in the United States, it is sometimes hard not to bend our students' interests in the direction where money and prestige lie – and if money lies in the practical application of specialties, prestige commonly lies in the driest possible pursuit of the same specialties on a more abstract level. But even when we are free of such entanglements, we must hope for the sort of purity of heart that can carry us beyond the timidity of conformism and even the bold pride of rebelliousness. For we must come to terms with the great works in a spirit of openness and humility; yet we must be willing to use every conceivable intellectual resource, even when we are not really qualified, that can possibly help us see what is happening; and then be glad (really glad, not just polite) when our colleagues, with a different command of resources, are able to correct us. More particularly, we must be willing to do a series of tasks, all of which are morally difficult.

We must be willing to respect the past and its great, to have faith in the rationality of mankind; very difficult in the face of daily experience. It may help us, to consider that the innumerable irrationalities tend to be random and so tend to cancel each other out, while only the occasional rationalities can be cumulatively meaningful; but fundamentally we require a more inward faith, the willingness to stake our efforts on the hope that something cherished by intelligent and sensitive people over many generations is at least unlikely to be trivial. Without this faith, the course of least resistance – at least when dealing with heritages not hedged with the loyalties we still owe our own (there, perhaps, we face the opposite problem!) – is to write off a history like Abulfazl's, despite the generations that admired and copied and treasured it, at the lowest available estimate, as so much toadying to a king, and count anything that seems to hint otherwise as mere coincidence. But if we have faith enough to explore the improbable and discover its own rationale, then we must be willing to let the work we deal with sound strange to Modern ears – and we must be willing to be identified with it, and so sound strange along with it: a task perhaps more difficult than the first. But to be willing to trust the alien even if we ourselves seem to become alien in the process must be implemented, if it is to have sound results (for it is just the opener scholars who may romanticize), by the willingness to take nothing in the work at hand for granted, but to pursue painstakingly every point where a difficulty can arise. And this means a willingness to use all the resources humanly available, whether one has been previously trained in them or not; and then to bring to the work a responsiveness to new total visions of what it can mean to be human. Finally, most difficult of all, to cut one's losses when proved wrong and start over again.

What is astonishing is that so many scholars have indeed proved willing and reasonably able to do all this. For it seems very hard to teach it in school, save by contagion from one scholar to another. We must, fundamentally, count on this contagion continuing among us. But perhaps we can give it some institutional support. We need the specialisms and their watchdogs, the university departments. But the pride and the narrow persistence which are both needed to maintain those specialisms drag against the courage and the openness and the humility which we require for our purposes. Hence it will be well if, in our universities as well as outside them, countervailing institutional forms can be set up alongside, where the pressures will be to transcend the limitations of specialisms. Such forms are not easy to devise, but the Committee on Social Thought may form something of a model, to look no further.

If we are able to maintain, and perhaps even enlarge, the moral resources of our scholarship, then we may be able to develop an ever fuller appreciation of the great pre-Modern heritages, which can have two consequences. It can afford an essential perspective upon our Modern life, so largely determined as it is by its special conditions of massive multiple technical specializations. And it may allow us to build more mutual respect, and to alleviate the fears that have arisen, between the heirs of the several heritages – short of simply eliminating those heritages altogether, which is the Gordian solution of certain revolutionaries. In particular, as we learn how best to allow the ancient classics to speak to all Moderns, we may learn better to ease the mistrust of Modern non-Westerners, such as Muslims, toward the West – a mistrust accentuated by the peculiar, if limited, role that the Western heritage has played in giving technical Modernity the form in which Muslims have had to assimilate it. And correspondingly, as the range of classics accessible for Westerners is broadened beyond the Occident, we may help Westerners out of their parochialism, and make them more capable of a genuinely human, and not merely regional, cultural leadership; such as they alone, by fortunate circumstances, seem to have the material and moral leisure to exercise.

2. The Classics in Translation: Their Place in a Modern Education

by

DAVID GRENE

"Greek scholars are privileged people; few of them know Greek and none of them know anything else". So says Adolphus Cousins, the Professor in *Major Barbara* which Shaw wrote at the beginning of this century. The jibe represents a measure of truth about the study of Greek literature at any time. It is peculiarly true of what it had become between the Renaissance and the twentieth century; it is out of this condition of classical education that emerge both the present state of the usual classical department of a university in England or the United States and any new project for making something else of it.

What Shaw is saying is that you cannot tell whether a professor of Greek knows Greek in the same sense that you can be certain of the proficiency of a professor of a modern language; and that his skill or knowledge in classics (of whatever calibre it may be) apparently releases him from the necessity of knowing anything in the Western tradition about those subjects of which Greek and Latin literature treates. The scholar of Plato, Cousins means, is not expected to know anything of the later history of philosophy, nor the expert in Aeschylus anything about Shakespeare or Ibsen. This was almost true in the period of the hundred years before the First World War – in Britain anyway. It has not quite ceased to be true to-day, though the direction of classical studies, in the ordinary academic department, is somewhat different. To-day it has become one more exotic subject on the university curriculum, on a par with Egyptology. Its cut-offness nowadays is due not to the privileged position it enjoys – or, if so, only vestigially – but rather to its loneliness and lack of students.

What is true of the peculiar position of Greek in modern education is true in much the same degree of Latin. When we speak of these two as dead languages, what do we mean? Not only that the languages are not spoken as French and German are. We mean that the fragments of the two literatures which we possess constitute all the relevant linguistic material available. It is entirely possible for a single man to have read every scrap of classical Greek and Latin literature several times over. Knowing a modern language means understanding it as a living unpredictable entity, with which the speaker is in a partly unconscious harmony. The dead languages can be completely *learned*. There is just so much of them and, with greater or lesser sensitivity on the part of the learner, what there is of them can be known. Their life is confined to the existent texts. Thus we cannot be sure that the Greek professor is in harmony with the ancient language. He may be only a plodding fellow who knows everything there is in the fragments – and let us bear in mind that what we have is only a relatively small amount of what was written. He learned these texts originally from other men and from translation: therefore, through the medium of his own tongue. We do not even know exactly how ancient Greek sounded. The intimacy of its rhythms is in part denied us. Hence the first part of Shaw's jeer "Few of them know Greek".

It is true that both Greek and Latin literature have extensions of life. There is mediaeval Latin and Byzantine Greek. In some universities in Britain to-day there is an inclination to take in both Byzantine and modern Greek along with the classical language in a study of the total life of Greek literature. But what the classics has always been hitherto – and that means what it has signified to each generation since the Renaissance – has been a large fragment of literature covering roughly nine hundred years from Homer in 750 B.C. to Marcus Aurelius at the end of the second century A.D.

This unique body of literature, limited in scope and isolated from our more passionate knowledge by our ignorance of its spoken sounds, became, particularly in the eighteenth and nineteenth centuries and particularly in Britain, almost liturgical in character as far as education was concerned. A thorough grounding in it was believed to ensure the proper kind of temper in a man, the proper appreciation of *style*, moral and aesthetic, and the proper standard of values, both in general and in detail. It was the training of judges and colonial governors as well as school-masters and journalists and writers. In a more vestigial form it was a pre-requisite for soldiers and doctors and lawyers. One must admit that it worked remarkably well.

It was liturgical in character. The object was not in the main, and certainly not at an advanced level, to establish anything new about the subject treated. Research was carried on as a sort of private hobby of classical professors. Classical scholarship meant primarily the possession of *know-*

ledge of the Greek and Latin texts and the passing on of this knowledge to others was the public usefulness of the classical scholar. His aim in teaching was to imbue the mind of his pupils with something of the atmosphere which he himself had found significant or almost sacred. Some of the means to this end may now seem to you so remote as to be funny. I was trained in this tradition, though it was then in its last days, and I remember on an examination having to write in Greek iambics (the verse of Greek tragedy) a version of "To be or not to be". What was required ideally was to think oneself into the mind of Sophocles saying the words of Shakespeare .What it amounted to was to find, in one's moments of inspiration, those Greek words, phrases and metrical turns which, as they lingered in one's head from the reading of Sophocles, made the most effective communication with the ideas provoked by the passage of Shakespeare. The furthest extension of ingenuity, and perhaps the most interesting educationally, took place when one came up against an idea or concept which clearly would not have occurred to Sophocles. Then, as my professor of composition told us, "we must imagine what a Greek would have said if such an idea had occurred to him".

In this older classical education, in universities, the use of translations had no place. What the student must do was recreate in his mind linguistically some image of the original word and the original sentence. The critical appraisal of what it meant or how it was related to other meanings could come afterwards or perhaps not come at all. For to be able to *construe* was in itself partly making one again a citizen of Greece or Rome. The merits of the system were its unselfconscious concentration on style and words. Its achievements in the formation of an educated taste were tremendous; in inducing clarity and sharpness of critical judgement they were also great. But it may be doubted whether it did so well when conveying the explicit meaning of the classical past as literature, philosophy or history. And it is in this direction, or nowhere, that modern education needs the classics. The student *must* try – and the effort must be really made possible for him – to gain immediate access to the meaning of the Greek tragedies, the epics of Homer, the history of Herodotus and Thucydides, the philosophy of Plato and Aristotle, the poems of Virgil, Catullus and Lucretius, and the history of Tacitus.

This meaning cannot be of the kind that would have been natural to those men's contemporaries. Too much of the thought of Western literature has grown directly out of classical literature to permit such a directly historical approach as this. It is not necessary, though it can be a pleasant pursuit, to try to establish with greater exactness the order of the Platonic dialogues or the facts behind the narrative of Thucydides or the changes in the physical structure of the theatre between Aeschylus and Euripides. All of these inquiries have value but it is, as far as the educational purposes of classical teaching go, a secondary value. Those who pursue such subjects are treating classical literature exactly as though it were any other record of man's adventures on this earth in the past – as though it were the history of Egypt or China.

Inquiry into any subject precise enough to be regarded academically, naturally has rules of its own and the continued life of the inquiry depends on turning up something new – that has not been previously discovered. But newness in classical education is something different from this. For the western world it is the record of the two peoples from whom our whole system of thought, in aesthetics, metaphysics and politics, stems. It is the relation of the fundamental classical works to what has followed them and challenged them on the same lines that matters to us. T. S. Eliot says somewhere that every great work of literature changes in its meaning when another of the same order and with some significant relationship to it is produced. The Iliad is different for us, has, within limits, a different meaning from what it had for the early nineteenth century because of the creation of Tolstoy's *War and Peace* and Joyce's *Ulysses*. The criticism of history and literature and philosophy is a sifting of the questions repeatedly raised at different angles, a study of the dialogue of authors of the same kind across the ages.

Classics does not belong or certainly does not solely belong in a modern university as a separated discipline, which is now the best that happens to it in most places. Nor is it the sole body of humanistic work as it was for the centuries between the Renaissance and the eighteenth. But it is *the very core of our knowledge of western man* and it must be *sought again in each generation* as the new works which challenge its propositions or its answers throw new light on their meaning and implications. It was the ignoring of this which made Shaw say of the Greek scholar "None of them know anything else." The kind of man criticized was one who knew Plato well, but cared nothing for Kant, who would compare Homer with Virgil but neither with Milton, would read Aeschylus with enjoyment but would never wonder out loud for the benefit of his pupils about the remarkable difference of this sort of tragedy and that of Shakespeare or Ibsen.

For use in this central position in humanistic education the classics *must* be taught in translation. All students specializing in advanced work in the literature, history and philosophy of the western world ought to have a thorough knowledge of the basic classical works in these fields. A more elementary knowledge is certainly desirable in the general education of those who are either going no further in academic specialization or are specializing in other branches. But whether one is thinking of advanced students, though not specialists in classics, or general education, obviously far the most of the teaching must be done through translation. It would be a quite impossible task, in point of time, to teach the Greek and Latin languages really well to the quantities of students concerned, and a proposition of this kind would be so unpopular as to render any approach to it also unacceptable. The important point to realize indeed is that only an almost perfect command of the two languages would be decisively better for the purposes I have mentioned than teaching through translations. It is possible – I have done it on occasion – to bring beginning students within the first two years to a fair linguistic knowledge so that they can read Homer and some Sophocles and Plato with appreciation. I am very far from undervaluing such instruction. But for the broad training of which we have been speaking, it will not do. The response *must* be more immediate than that which attends the laborious deciphering of the grammatical structure, even after two years of work. And the relatively large amount of writing – if classical antiquity has only left us a fragment it is still a large fragment – could not be assimilated. It is doubtful, I believe, whether even in the greatest days of classical education in England in the nineteenth century the student, with nearly twelve years spent on Greek and Latin, between school and college, attained such proficiency. I mean that I doubt whether during his college career he was in a position to have a deep or direct understanding of the texts. I think that his schooling and college training gave him an excellent linguistic knowledge, but that only the most exceptional student ever consciously asked himself what this play of Sophocles or that of Aeschylus had to say about man's sense of tragedy. They were certainly not taught to think in such terms. They were not so examined and the overwhelming balance of their time was spent in concentration on the letter rather than the meaning of what they read. I mean this to include the exegesis of textual and grammatical difficulties, and later, especially nearer our own times, the discussion of historical, archaeological and anthropological problems which still do not bear on the central significance of the work examined.

The case against the teaching of classics in translation in universities is often absurdly overstated. Of course, no translation is the same thing as the original. Of course, this decline is sharpest in the case of lyric poetry, with verse plays and epics next most difficult and the prose expository works relatively easier. But surely the overwhelming probability is that modern readers can assimilate much of the original classics in English or whatever their native language is, though clearly there are different degrees of suitability among modern languages for rendering the classics. No one would seriously maintain that it is better not to read Tolstoy or Ibsen unless you read them in Russian or Norwegian, I doubt if many would even argue that it is better to read neither Dante nor Goethe unless in Italian or German. The whole experience of the past is against any such pedantic position. The seventeenth century is certainly soaked in the sense of classical models and classical examples. In England, at any rate, it is certain that the most potent source of these was Chapman's Homer, North's Plutarch, Dryden's versions of Homer and Virgil and the later Latin poets, and Hobbes' Thucydides. These were all translations made by great writers. They made them because presumably they wanted to express in an immediately apprehensible form the works of art they themselves enjoyed so profoundly. Even when, as then, classics occupied almost the whole of humanistic education except for some training in Hebrew and the Old Testament, most of the influence of classical literature, its widest diffusion, was through translation.

It is this model of the seventeenth century educated reader that should concern us today – allowing for all the difference of the two periods – when we think of classical training in translation in the universities. What we need to convey is the major impact of a play of Sophocles, the effect of both story and style in Homer, a feeling for the harshness and clarity of Thucydides. Much of this I am sure can come across in translation. Even some of the purer poetic qualities, more difficult to render, can yield surprisingly to an inspired effort in reproduction. One of the most extraordinary successes in recent years has been Day Lewis' translation of the Aeneid and the Georgics.

The real danger in basing modern education in classics on translation lies in the simplification of the issues. The case for translation is that one wants to teach the student what the play or the poem or the history *means* and not only what it says. This is indeed the true argument. But it is easy to interpret it as an excuse for sloppy thinking, vagueness and the false assimilation of old concepts to new. In the first place it is essential that teachers of classical literature in translation should know the original languages themselves really well. Otherwise there is no brake on critical interpretation and the errors are compounded. What is gained by the knowledge of the originals is the sense where the ancients are *different* from us as well as where they have matter in common with us. Without a thorough grasp of the difference of the classical civilisation and our own the instruction loses all body. Both in instruction and in reading translations the student must never be allowed to lose sight of *what was individual and unique in that Graeco-Roman world,* for our understanding of that difference is a part of the educational process.

It is a mistake, for instance, to deduce large economic theories from the life of classical antiquity in face of the total defect of satisfactory evidence. It is a mistake to ignore the way in which a concern with personality is a modern phenomenon. To use our modern concept of personality to shed light on the ancient world is to distort your conclusions. It is a mistake to underestimate the extent to which Christianity altered the preconceptions with which we approach the subject of religion, in comparison with the classical Greek and Roman. This is how things go wrong when teaching through translation is too lightheartedly accepted. *These are the occasion of valid objections to what is called popularization of the classics.*

This wrong popularization takes the form of a series of ideological errors against which every modern teacher of classics must guard – and in spite of this every one of us makes them all the time, because, if one feels the immediacy of the texts, it is exceedingly hard to prevent this sense of immediacy from making a too hasty marriage with the general ideas which one is breathing in at every moment from one's own present. The professor who is teaching in the original language spends so much time and energy establishing exactly what the text says that, even if reasonably scrupulous, he will hardly feel he has to produce some all embracing theory to account for its meaning. He will feel that he has done a day's work when both he and those whom he teaches know what the words say. Both the student and his teacher in the regular classics department have an impersonal cut and dried task before them where the significant values, if they come at all, do so by implication. The need to be explicit drives many of us to ex-plaining ideas and meanings from classical literature in a facile modern form because it is what the majority of the students would like to hear and is eager to assimilate. And not yielding to this particular temptation leaves the teacher frequently with the uncomfortably bare consciousness that he does not in fact know what his author is trying to say! This discomfort the old fashioned teacher of classics could keep safely at bay for most of his lifetime.

The temptation to interpret in modern concepts grows greater for the translator as distinct from the teacher, and particularly for the translator of imaginative works. Here the intermediary, the translator, is not dealing directly with issues but with the stylistic character of the play or poem as a whole. He is trying not only to render the literal meaning of the words,

their naked communication value, as though this were a chemist's pre-
scription or a railway guide. He is concerned with the sub-values of words
and phrases. Inevitably the translation he is writing assimilates itself to
some extent to that contemporary model which he feels is closest to his
original. There is nothing wrong with this. In fact, if he is a sensitive man
and his notion of the resemblance is correct, this constitutes one of the
reasons that the translation may be important – because the modern
world demands to see the classical work in a certain approximation of its
own terms. This contemporary model is the mould of thought and expression which we understand and into it must be poured the character
of the original.

But the key words are "a certain approximation"; there are for instance
passages in Aeschylus and Sophocles where almost any conscientious
translator knows that the thought in its dramatic effect cannot be con-
veyed adequately through the English stage conventions. Sometimes this
is because what was commonplace in the rendering of emotion in their
theater is bizarre in ours or vice versa. At such times there is an irresistible
urge to replace what is uncouth, and therefore spoils the effect, by something facile and acceptable. This is where the translator must make his
mistake on the side of clumsiness rather than imaginative fluency. The
text does not *say* the easy thing. That rendering of emotion which appears
to us so dislocated and impossible may mean an approach to understanding which we cannot grasp. But we can at least put the bare bones of
the enigmatic meaning before the reader. Perhaps at some other time,
someone specially gifted in our own, with only the bones to help him, can
resurrect the living animals. He will not do so if we pawn off on him a
totally different dummy beast nicely stuffed. It may be that this is a twentieth century phenomenon – in some way our special sense of the sacred-
ness of history. In the great age of translation, in the seventeenth century,
Dryden at the end and Chapman at the beginning used their enormous
original poetic gifts to express the inner sense of their classical authors
without too finnicky a concern with the exact form of the meaning. It
seems to me that we cannot do that without violating our integrity.

It is sometimes said, simply or cleverly, that the change in later western
civilisation is such that the ideas that come to us from the vanished classical
world have no relevance, and that our aesthetic experience of it is based
on arbitrary assumptions which may be entirely false. I think this is untrue.
In some way the response of our imagination to Greek and Latin literature,
especially Greek, is very natural and unforced. I have ventured to close this
paper by selecting two examples of tragic situation from the Greek theatre

to put before you, as an illustration of what seems to me an immediate relevance of their thinking to ours. I must make the discussion very short and the outlining of the dramatic situation must necessarily be crude.

The first comes from the Oresteia of Aeschylus. This extraordinary play or series of plays (since it is our only example of a trilogy) deals with the question of guilt, in various forms. Agamemnon was killed by his wife Clytemnestra because he had sacrificed their daughter Iphigeneia to appease the God that had prevented the sailing of his fleet to Troy. To revenge his father's murder the boy Orestes kills his mother, being incited to this by Apollo. The Furies pursue him, Apollo defends him. Athena speaks as arbiter, representing Zeus. The weight of the play in its inner feeling bears on the nature of guilt considered as a factor in a developing situation.

If Agamemnon is forced by the God's actions to sacrifice his daughter, what is his guilt? If Clytemnestra is God's agent in murdering her husband, what is her guilt? If Orestes revenges his father under Apollo's orders, what is his guilt? And yet all three characters act with different degrees of willingness and awareness of what they are doing. Does this personal aspect of guilt mean something as against its objective significance in the moral universe? How to reconcile the free will of the humans to their subjection to the Divine design? The climax is to see the institution of the human court of the Areopagus created to try to separate the degrees of guilt, while the conflicting Divine agencies, Apollo and the Furies, find their appropriate place in the Athenian religious establishment. This play is somewhat as if on the modern stage one could produce a dramatic treatment of the theme of freedom, in a series of episodes starting with Adam and Eden and culminating in the establishment of the American constitution. The gigantic power of Aeschylus' imagination is revealed in his capacity to conceive of an eternal and universal principle moving through time and finding a significant moment of decision in a most prosaic human institution. The abstract and concrete are very strangely interwoven. This rendering where grotesqueness almost but not quite overwhelms the sublimity is very near to our imaginative demands.

The second example comes from the last two plays of Sophocles. In them the heroic figure, Philoctetes and the old Oedipus, is chosen for a final apocalypse in which his power will be decisive to whichever of two waring states he lends it. Both Philoctetes and Oedipus, during most of their lives, had been cursed and isolated from their fellow men by the same Gods that finally call them to their great destiny. Philoctetes had been marooned by his comrades on a desert island because they cannot endure the smell of his suppurating foot – he had been bitten by a snake when he accidentally violated one of the holy places. Oedipus had in self defence killed a man who proved to be his father and married the queen of Thebes who was his mother. Henceforth he had been an outlawed wanderer from the cities of men. In both plays the mysterious Divine power called them to a moment of greatness which forced them back into the world that had rejected them. In each play there are three forces working on the situation: the will of the Gods, altogether inexplicable in human terms and invincible; the religious sentiment of most men who readily follow the expressions of the Divine will – when they can learn it – without any checks of loyalty or affection when it turns them against their fellow man; and the lonely embittered frustrated strength of the chosen sinner-saint, who accepts perforce the decision of the Gods, but with the proud reservation of his own innocence, and the right of anger against those that have betrayed him. For us this integrity of the individual and the human absurdity of the circumstances that now depress and now elevate him is *our* climate of heroism.

3. Discussions of the Classics

In the discussion that followed these two papers, Yu-sheng Lin and Charles Morazé considered the desirability of developing a program in the Chinese classics as part of contemporary education.

Mr. Lin thought it important that Chinese culture should be presented through its greatest philosophers (he cited Confucius as an example) just as Western philosophy should be presented through its greatest philosophers. The first task of Western students is, of course, to study Western classics really well. In the words of Professor Grene, these classics are "the very core of our knowledge of Western man." So they are essential if a Western man is to know himself. However, on account of the inherent human desire for a genuine understanding of the self, and on account of the need for a world community, it would be insufficient to study Western classics alone. Mr. Lin suggested that the Western student's sense of identity could, in fact, best be sharpened by a sincere effort to understand one non-western culture. This effort would give him a new perspective in looking at his own cultural heritage and so enable him to examine himself in a fresh light. Furthermore, it would broaden his spiritual horizon and lead him to realize that the essence of a foreign culture is actually less alien than he supposed, because it reveals human values (albeit in a particular setting) that are common to all mankind.

Mr. Lin did not think it desirable for a Western student to study Chinese or any other foreign culture at the expense of understanding his own culture (as now is the case with the training sometimes offered in the new area studies in the universities in the United States). That is why he suggested that Westerners should be introduced to Chinese classics only in conjunction with the study of Western classics. Such a program would serve a double purpose related to world community. It would give a Western student both a deeper sense of his own particular identity and a closer feeling of communion with people of other cultures. The sense of human universalism could be thus evoked without losing the richness of cultural diversity, and such a combination of unity with diversity is, we all seem to feel at this meeting, a cornerstone for the edifice of a viable world community.

Mr. Lin thought it important too that Westerners become at home in the languages of China, and Chinese in one of the Western languages. In each case knowledge of language should be combined with appreciation of music, customs and visual art, an appreciation which would, he thought, also reveal basic values common to Asian and Western cultures.

Mr. Morazé pointed out that the structure of Chinese language is completely different from any Western language. It is easier, he remarked, for modern Europeans to understand ancient Greek, even though that presents immense difficulties, than to understand modern Chinese. While the difficulties of learning Greek and Latin had been presented by Mr. Grene as a reason for reading the Classics in translation, Mr. Morazé suggested that, in order to understand the modern Asian world, it is of the first importance to learn Chinese and to master Chinese forms of representation, precisely because the difficulties of translating Chinese are greater than the difficulties of translating Greek. There is no other way of putting ourselves in the place of the Chinese than by making their language a part of us.

Mr. Rosenberg suggested that, in a way, the matter of translation was the central issue of the conference, because of the contribution which a common understanding of language might make to world community. He pointed out that anyone influenced by James Joyce is already involved in a total humanistic linguistic.[1] He had also noticed, without possessing any knowledge of Greek, that a remarkable change had taken place during the past two or three generations in the character of translations from the Greek, both with respect to precision and with respect to the outlook of the translator on the content. Insofar as literature is concerned, Mr. Rosenberg saw no other way of crossing the existing cultural divisions into

1. This would seem a much more hopeful means of overcoming language barriers to world community than esperanto. The adoption of that would strip from language the rich allusions which make possible meaningful communication and contribute to the understanding of other peoples and other ages. In fact the craze for esperanto has been another manifestation of the dehumanization and mechanization with which mankind in recent times is threatened (ed.).

a kind of world ethnic culture, than by means of movements towards a total humanistic linguistic, movements which, it seemed to him, had already begun.

Mr. Squirru took up Mr. Rosenberg's reference to a world ethnic culture. It was obviously arrogant for Europeans and Americans – whether of the north or south – to treat the classics only in terms of Western classics. As had been shown, there are Arabic classics and Chinese classics, and to steep the superior Western student in these, at the same time that the superior Arab and Oriental student is steeped in other classics than those of *his* own culture, offers one road towards world community. The concept of a world university had been raised repeatedly in the work of the Center for Human Understanding. If universities are to profit from that concept in breeding men capable of living in a world ethnic culture, it seems proper, both from the point of view of time and of common sense, to start with your own tradition but also to open doors to other great traditions, as Mr. Hodgson had suggested in his paper.[1]

Mr. Hodgson stressed the immense difficulties and complications inherent in the attempt to bring the whole world together culturally through a comprehensive treatment of the classics. He suggested a possible way of making a beginning. Some kind of certificate could be awarded by a private (not a governmental) body, perhaps within an existing university or universities. Such a certificate would not be for a culture which drew equally on all our human classical heritages, in a diffuse manner. It would be a certificate for genuine competence in *two* of the major cultural heritages. Such a competence obviously could not be expected of everyone. A candidate for it would have to be exceptionally gifted. A serious competence would be expected of him in two classic strands of our human heritage, including in each case the candidates' own heritage. Such a training could grow naturally out of the experience of both the Committee on Social Thought and the Center for Human Understanding. It might develop as an educational norm for those people who would like to become real world citizens.

---

1 See above, III, 1.

PART IV: THE PURSUIT OF BEAUTY

Mr. Rosenberg's evocation of a world ethnic culture [1] led him on to explore the question of international communication, not as had been already sketched by means of formal education in the classics, but by the work of the architect and the craftsman. He considered that it is inherently easier to communicate, across cultural barriers, through the visual arts than through literature, because of the difficulties of translation.

Already in connection with the discussion of possible contributions of the physical sciences to community, Mr. Squirru had evoked, by his intervention, the need for communication through the mysteries of art, both visual and poetic. Mr. Rosenberg and Mr. Bourbon Busset brought the discussion into these realms and Mr. Squirru then pursued the theme.

1. Visual Internationalism: Promise or Threat?

by

HAROLD ROSENBERG

In the visual arts – that is, in painting and sculpture, and also in motion pictures – international understanding on a certain level is an achieved fact. Artists from anywhere communicate with one another more readily than with their grandmothers. Modern western culture has actually become an eclectic culture even though it has retained certain central ideals.

The same is true of all the other cultures in their actual operations to-

1. See above, pp. 80–81.

day. International exhibitions of contemporary art reveal a continual exchange of styles, and while it is true that this has always been so with cultures, we have the new factor of an almost simultaneous exchange. So
there is no time for separate development, even if anyone were inclined
towards such a development. In an international show at Venice or São
Paulo, one sees the same motifs repeated by artists from all regions of the
world. An Arab, for instance, will present paintings based on Jackson
Pollock. A Japanese is involved with Mondrian. (We have to keep in mind,
of course, that the western artist discovered these other cultures often
before the other cultures discovered the western artists).

There is no terribly unfair western advantage about this. The new kind of
artistic exchange has been initiated and it probably has something to do
with commodity exchange and with the whole industrial complex, which
is both recent and historically novel. In other words, we are living in what
can be called *modern* culture, and it is from this standpoint perhaps that we
have to look at these problems of community, since the past itself has been
drawn into this vortex and now exists as a kind of simultaneous present.

Many of the problems that appear almost insurmountable to classical
scholars give way in the face of certain phenomena. Among these is the
universal museum in which essentially we all live culturally, and from
which we pick out whatever it is that attracts us, regardless of where we
find it. This of course is especially true of artists, but since we have already
been in this position – which I have called the tradition of the new – for a
century it cannot be regarded as a completely transitory phenomenon. It
has become a condition in which we actually are functioning now, even
though many institutions don't quite realize this, perhaps for certain self-
defensive reasons. We don't have to go into that. I am simply trying to give a
phenomenological account of where we are in regard to some of the questions of world organization, world culture.

The so-called international style of the early twentieth century, which
is to be found in buildings throughout the world, whether they are government buildings or airports, has now evolved into a global art. You all
know from experience that if you are set down at an airport and are not
told where you are, and if you then take a bus into the city, you have to
get to your hotel before you know in which city you are. So let us start
with this uniformity which some people think has still to be achieved.

In the course of this development, local, national and regional styles
have been absorbed. The same thing is true of the handicrafts. Today there
are international congresses of handicrafters. You usually think of a craft as
an extremely vestigial kind of activity conducted by isolated peasants or

people in backward countries. However, this is not the case. The handicraft people are now in constant touch with each other. They have an international magazine, international organizations.[1]

Unfortunately this has tended to produce something called "airport-craft". Still people seem to like it, because the customer also has this kind of international taste, and does not really care very much whether what he buys in the airport was made in Bali or by some Tennessee mountaineer. There is a kind of "handicraft style" which communicates itself in much the same way as a fine arts style.

In other words, what we are talking about, in one sense, is the negative power of modern art in breaking down parochialism, on all fronts. The Japanese influenced western art in the 19th century, the Africans influenced it in the 20th century; pre-Columbian art is practically as familiar in the art magazines as Picasso, and Picasso himself has something to do with African art. The whole thing is an enormous mélange. These are processes which have already taken place and probably are the bases from which we should begin to think about our problems, instead of behaving as if we were still in the Victorian age observing with a degree of horror the breakdown of tradition. All traditions have already been so mangled, and so mingled together, that we are actually talking about a new cultural situation of a nonregional character.

Not only has provincialism been broken down in regard to place, but also in relation to time. When we speak of new art today, we are also speaking about the art that is constantly being excavated by archaeologists and which is being brought into focus through critical analysis and historical research. This work is immediately translated into a communicable form by means of reproductions and slides, and becomes part of the vocabulary of every student. The fact is that in art schools in this country – I don't think the situation is much better elsewhere – the students, art students, very rarely see many actual paintings unless they happen to be in New York or Paris or London. They study art through slides. This is even more true of art historians, who by this time do not even care to look at paintings. I mean, they regard an actual painting as a distraction in their effort to establish the evolution of styles, so they don't have anything to do with that!

We know, for example, that M. Malraux, the French Minister of Culture, has suggested the printing and wide distribution of the one hundred best works of Western painting, so that everybody would be able to have them

1. See the relation of this to the proposals for a renewal of handicraft in Nef, *The United States and Civilization*, pp. 360–61.

around and absorb them, without necessarily thinking about them. By the way, I don't intend that as a sarcastic remark. Quite the opposite. I think the presence of works of art is much more important to people than the ideas which tend to accompany them. So I want to emphasize that the idea of having pictures available without comment is, in my mind, often preferable to having them around with comment, particularly the kind of comment now made available by certain museums where you pick up a little receiver and it tells you what the picture is about.

Our own tradition, as a result, has been placed in the completely human context. We cannot look at a Giotto or listen to Bach any more without being aware of the total culture in which they appear. For example, in music, the developments introduced by Schoenberg have made it possible to transcribe ethnic music in a way that could not be done with the techniques available in nineteenth century western music. Schoenberg's "twelve-tone row" has provided a vocabulary for translation of the music of non-Western cultures on a most fantastic level, a new kind of accuracy, a new, non-restricted kind of hearing. The senses of the contemporary public are being transformed constantly by the availability of kinds of art which could not be understood before, and which were rejected automatically by the eye or the ear trained in the conventions of the European tradition. Today we have a new kind of approach to objects, a new approach to sound, which is of enormous bearing on the whole question of what is going to happen to any local or national culture.

In sum, an international vocabulary has already developed which is accessible to individuals everywhere. Even the totalitarian countries have felt its impact. The Soviet Union has had trouble with vanguard art ever since it was founded, and this disturbance keeps cropping up. There seems to be no way in which you can keep these mushrooms down. Periodically it becomes a political issue of the first importance. In the other east-European countries, there is a very vigorous activity which finds no difficulty in passing over the Iron Curtain. You have Polish abstract artists; you have a great deal of activity in Yugoslavia. In fact, some Yugoslavs have already come to tell us how backward we are in our conceptions of painting.

A concrete example of the new globalism is a show I saw last spring in New York put on by the Kingdom of Kuwait, which is, as you know, one of the Arabian countries. They have got very rich apparently, so about six years ago they decided that since they had now got into the world exchange financially, it was time for them to have an art movement. So the Minister of Culture picked a group of fellows, sent them to Paris, and within six years they put on this exhibition in New York and said, "Now, after only six years we already have modern art." They even had one fellow who had been somewhat influenced by Delaunay, although I doubt that he'd seen very much of his work. He produced a lot of abstract circular forms which retained, however, indications of mythological demons from the Kuwaiti tradition. His idea was, "If you're going to have new art, you've got to have a new art movement." So he presented himself as the father of a new art movement which he called "Circlism." He was the only circlist in Kuwait and presumably in the world. But you can see that the spirit of being a vanguardist with an art movement had been authentically absorbed by him, undoubtedly in trying to get rid of those ferocious female demons who were gobbling up the Kuwait male heroes!

In fact, it is possible that, in art, international exchange may have gone too far. This is what Marshall Hodgson, in another line of thought, seems to be worrying about. I mean, in the sense referred to by Professor Stone, too; that is, a neglect of the need to know oneself, which is one of our "prejudices" inherited from the Greeks, a prejudice that we need to preserve. I think it would be very unfortunate if we dumped that idea, which doesn't take much scholarship to feel, because it has come down to us by the mysterious means that culture uses to transmit basic insights.

The new world culture that we're talking about has a tendency to be oriented completely towards the present – and the future. Its concept of what is going on is not based on a continuation of the past, but on expectations. Those artists you see in the international shows, who have chosen to work in this manner or that manner, make their choice on the basis of an anticipation of what art is going to be. Nobody says "What has art been?" since this is irrelevant. The issue is "What is art going to become"?

Consequently the artists, and the collectors, and, above all, the curators, gamble on their prediction of the future. This, of course, reflects the condition in which we all are. We are all gambling on historical prediction – the government is gambling on it, the universities are gambling on it in their plans for expansion. Stockbrokers and businessmen we need not mention! So art too has become a gambling on the future rather than a continuation of the past or a manifestation of loyalty to a particular tradition. This is one of the great wrenching issues in contemporary art. Instead of *asserting* values, people tend to gamble on the potential victory of values which may not be their own, but which show a likelihood of coming out on top. That is a very passive human attitude, and I should say it is not a very good one.

But there are certain forces that press artists – and, as I said, collectors and to an even greater extent museum curators – in this direction. For example, in becoming a global medium, art tends to separate itself from the concerns of the artist as an individual. He becomes a technician of style, a supplier of materials for the bureaucracies of modernization which have sprung into being throughout the world. The effect is to separate art from moral and social concerns, as we saw in our first two sessions science and technology tend to become separated from them. Art-historical consciousness replaces the consciousness of man's needs, and art-historical motives replace social and spiritual purpose. The terrible threats to man's existence are ignored in the contemplation of the evolution of aesthetic styles; as we heard in the first session of this conference scientists might consider that the development of their science is the first consideration in viewing a military or a political problem.[1] The individual artist feels helpless in the face of the intellectual appropriation of his product. He is unable to resist the demands of the controllers of his medium.

Thus globalism becomes another force propelling the arts toward dissolution into mass communication and mass entertainment. That is a problem we see in all the capitols of art today. This grim outlook darkens the enlightened passage towards world community. The situation may be one which the individual cannot affect, though there's nothing to prevent him from criticizing it and from privately creating the sort of art that satisfies him.

It is in this private choice that the link of art today with the art of the past is maintained. Art deals with the reality of helplessness. Tragedy is its primary form. In Freud's terms, art arises from an inability to act effectively in the real world. That the artist can act in his work, while accepting defeat elsewhere and even the defeat of the world, makes him optimistic by nature and enables him to look the dismal facts in the face. All creators believe in miracles, including the miracle of world peace.

1. Cf. above, pp. 15 ff., esp. pp. 20–21.

2. Letters and Nationalism

by

JACQUES DE BOURBON BUSSET

I think that the problem with which we are dealing is in fact a problem of communication. And I rather wonder if we might not help to clarify it by recognizing that when we have a message to convey, two matters need to be kept in mind. First the spread of the message. Second, its comprehension.

You can have a very rich message for few people, or a very poor message for great numbers of peoples. I don't mean that one excludes the other absolutely, but I think there is a kind of relation between the extension and the comprehension of a message; that the spread, beyond a certain point, tends to deform and dilute the message.

(I am speaking under the scrutiny of Mr. Anderson, who is looking at me with a very critical eye probably because he considers me one of those men of letters who tries to make comparisons with natural science in order to appear more serious!) But I think that when we speak about art and literature the generalization I have made becomes clear. Mr. Rosenberg has demonstrated this in a most brilliant manner. I am not referring to the whole of his talk but to those aspects of it where he showed that the wide multiplication of visual art tends to diminish the quality of the art that is disseminated. The same is true of music.

When one speaks about literature, the matter is more complicated, because you haven't got the immediate impact of the picture or the music. Of course neither the visual artist nor the man of letters seeks the extension of his message as his primary aim. That would be fatal. An artist – whether painter, writer or musician – whose purpose in his work is to reach a great number of people will kill his art with his own hands. That is quite clear.

It is the same with the scientist. The scientist doesn't seek to spread his message. That doesn't interest him a bit. What the scientist is attached to

is truth, and the discovery of truth. Whether what he discovers is afterwards communicated, whether it is communicated on a vast scale, is
another question. That doesn't concern him. It isn't his problem.

Speaking as a man of letters, I must say the matter is complicated, because the writer *does* wish to have his message understood. I mean that he
probably wouldn't write if he was absolutely convinced that he wouldn't
have a single reader. In fact, he is writing for one man, an unknown
reader, to whom he attributes all the qualities he would like to have himself. I think that is the real motivation of the writer. And if he thinks of
extensions beyond that one man, he's killed, he's dead, he's finished as a
writer.

In this reference to one man, I am not speaking of a deviation which I
think is common to all arts. According to that deviation, writers write for
writers, poets sing for poets, painters paint for painters, musicians compose
for musicians, belonging to the same little chapel, and even – what is most
extraordinary of all – critics write for critics, but for critics of their own
chapel too. That provides no basis for comprehension. What I actually
mean by the word comprehension is a very deep and intimate link between
the creator and the consumer, who is neither a colleague nor a rival,
even if the consumer he has in mind is only one person.

In view of these remarks, you may think it odd that I was for four years in
charge of the cultural relations of France. I was the head of the cultural
section of the French Foreign Office.[1] My experience with the difficulties
of communicating through art, difficulties which Mr. Rosenberg has explained clearly, was extensive. I saw both the advantages and the draw-
backs of the present situation, to which he has drawn attention. There has
certainly been a great extension of the artist's message. That is an advantage
from many points of view. But it has disadvantages too, and these loom
especially large when you add the barrier of language, and the differences
in mentality which are a reflection of differences in language. You come to
recognize that all too often what you communicate is not what the writer
was trying to communicate.

Perhaps the greatest obstacle to authentic communication in the cultural
field, however, is political. The real difficulty is that everything in the field
of culture is done by governments. There is, of course, UNESCO. But
Mr. Morazé won't contradict me if I say that UNESCO is not an inter-

---

1. This was before the time of Malraux (to whom Rosenberg referred), when there was
no special minister of culture, and cultural relations were all subsidiary to the minister
of foreign affairs, the French equivalent of the United States secretary of state (ed.).

national   rnational agency, but an intergovernmental organization, run by ma   ticular and individual national governments.

Speaking   one who has had governmental responsibility, I must say that, whii   before and during my tenure of cultural relations, I was above al   entative of my nation. The same was true of my British colleagu   even truer in the case of the United States. The United States Int.   Service was especially nationalistic because it mixed up cultural   s and political information. This is quite a mistake, a mistake we   d because we were more divided and separate. But, in fact, all of us hac   me thing in mind. It was our duty to extend the knowledge of our na   culture. Our aim was purely a nationalistic one. This should be made   clear, and, to repeat, I speak as a responsible person who participated in   nationalism.

So you see how great are   political obstacles for common understanding in the intellectual f   . Cultural nationalism is probably one of the most difficult forms of n   nalism to deal with, and one of the most dangerous, because it is car   flaged by its appearance of international-mindedness.[1] I must say I   s in a better position to understand this because I had served before   political official in the Foreign Office. (This looks like a confession   it is one.) I worked for Robert Schuman when he was Foreign Mini   had in consequence, when I took charge of cultural relations, t'   perience of political responsibility. Through that experience, I had   me convinced that we are living in a world where the only reality   national state. There is no international life. There is an internatiop   rit; there are private international organizations which are importar   it there is no international policy. The United Nations Organizati   only a juxtaposition of national states where no international   is actually at work. In the opinions the spirit may occasionally cro   perhaps, but not in the facts with which officials deal.

Tha   e conclusion I had come to before I was director of cultural relat   having become a kind of specialist in summit conferences. I do   ow how many I attended. In the process I decided that, in fact, the o   ning that was important was the personality of the decision makers.

          have considered the atomic bomb in our discussions, and I was very

n later discu   ith Mr. Rosenberg, Mr. Bourbon Busset agreed that nationality is
mething ve   erent from nationalism, and the group at the conference were in general agre   t with both men, that nationality, unlike the pride and assertiveness inherent   onalism, are by no means a handicap to world cultural community. Nationali   s conflict but, as Mr. Rosenberg argued (citing Melville's experiences as a sailo   d the globe), while there are many sources of conflict, the conflict has us   nothing to do with *nationality* (ed.).

much interested in what Mr. Anderson said. But the thing you need to remember is that only one man decided what should be done with the bomb. He could listen to the scientists; he could listen to the generals; he could listen to the admirals; he could listen to Churchill. But one man had somehow to take the decision to do it. As he explains clearly in his memoirs, that man was Mr. Truman.

That's the fact we mustn't forget, for this is the root and the explanation of all international policy. You can't escape the relevance of this fact to the present situation. I expect Mr. Douglas, who has had much governmental responsibility, will not disagree.

And I would add, with reference to the bomb, something Mr. Anderson did not say. Before the decision was taken, a plan had been consummated for the invasion of Japan. But why? Why was it necessary to invade Japan? Because of an arrangement made earlier between the American and the Russian governments. According to that agreement, three months after the capitulation of Germany, Russia was bound to enter the war against Japan. That meant a deadline on August 8th.[1] It was felt to be necessary for the United States to have the capitulation of Japan to prevent Russia from entering the far-eastern war. This was because experience with the Russian occupation of Germany was such as to disincline the United States from having Russia also participate in the occupation of Japan.

So you see again that the real factor in the decision was national and political. There was also, I would add, a question of personal relations between the heads of state, in this case between Stalin and Truman. You cannot say they felt great confidence in one another. I simply point this out to show that at the root of everything decisive is the question of the personal relations between the leading men in the world.

I would suggest in conclusion that what is important, and about this I speak again from my own experience, is the intellectual and moral values that guide the people at the top. That is the only thing which counts. And it is the only thing we can have no influence on, or very little. The picture is completely changed if these people have a great sense of integrity. That is the point.

And so I would end this perhaps somewhat confused statement by saying, rather paradoxically, that what led me, deeply motivated, to retire from the foreign service and from all official functions was my growing conviction that, when you are a high civil servant in no matter what country, you are tarred with the same brush. It is so for all. There are no exceptions. You are simply a cog in a process, the process of nationalism and the defense of the national interest.

1. 1945.

It will take a long time to change this. What is important, in waiting and hoping for that time, what people should be convinced of, is that the character of the man who has the ultimate responsibility is the vital factor.

So the only thing I thought I could do was to give this kind of personal testimony, by turning to what is for me the most congenial of occupations, that of letters, in its most personal and autobiographical form. I found I was convinced of only one thing: The real source of action at the highest level, by the man who makes the vital decisions, is the richness of his inner life. If he is simply a politician with no intellectual concerns, without real sensitivity, or valued beliefs rooted in personal reflection, he is worth nothing. So the writer should be convinced, and should seek to convince others, of the value of an inner life of integrity.

When I speak of inner life I don't mean sentimental or spiritual or religious only, but the intellectual, personal effort to be somebody. I would end by quoting from Mollâ Sadrà, as Mr. Hodgson did, when he said that the true philosopher has to renounce wealth, prestige (because that is how I understand status), conformity and rebelliousness. That is the absolute need of the statesman. I repeat, the only thing which is important is that we should be able to produce and select statesmen who would follow the model given a great many centuries ago by Mollâ Sadrà.

3. The Problem of Transcending Cultural Nationalism

by

RAFAEL SQUIRRU

I occupied a position in the Argentine Republic similar to that held earlier by Mr. Bourbon Busset in France. My experience concerning the handicaps to world community involved in government service tends to corroborate his. But, if I can follow the form of confession already adopted by two of the participants in this meeting, I would say that my resistance to the burden which led Bourbon Busset to resign was such that I never reached the point of resigning. I was literally kicked out by my own government! So my experience goes to bolster his statement that it is difficult to serve the interests of culture in the teeth of what some people consider national security.

I am glad to report that, in my case, nevertheless, the stand I made had some positive cultural value. It brought about a very pronounced reaction on the part of artists. After my dismissal, they paraded the streets and did such symbolic things as hanging pictures from the statue of our liberator, General San Martin. So, in spite of my dismissal, I was made to feel, not only that I had not done the wrong thing, but, thanks to the support I had received from men of culture in my country, that I had also done very much the right thing.

As circumstances turned out I was led to further positions of greater responsibility, and in a sense I hold a similar cultural job today in an international organization, the Pan-American Union. Needless to say, I might meet with a similar crisis in my present work, but as yet this has not happened.

For three years now I have been furthering what I consider to be primarily general and universal cultural interests. Only too often it is true, we feel cowed, in a sense, by the fact that other people who take on these responsibilities and who work for national political purposes, appear to have a bigger say than we have. We tend to think that perhaps it is *they* who are right. But I believe that men of culture have a responsibility to realize that there is no higher national interest than the cultural interest which transcends nationalism, and that when governments do not further that interest it is not because there is something wrong with culture, but because there is something wrong with the governments. I stress this point of view, because I believe that an adherence to it can provide at least a partial solution to some of the difficulties in the way of world community that we are trying to face here in this meeting of a Center for Human Understanding.

We in Latin America regard Mr. Rosenberg as one of the major art critics of the United States. The brilliant remarks of his, to which we have just listened, lead me to comment on the idea that, as a cultural manifestation, imitation is different from assimilation. I have in mind especially the problem of styles. Mr. Rosenberg explained very well how we can speak today of an international style. Now, this has a double edge to it.

The fact is that many feel the pressure to imitate what is given a high consideration, because it seems to be what the market demands. In so doing they betray, in a sense, their own authentic artistic integrity. They often renounce their own style, in order to be judged by what at the moment enjoys the greatest prestige. Of course, Mr. Rosenberg has already pointed to this danger. It is the same that has been touched on in these discussions, as besetting the historian, the philosopher, and the scientist, the danger of compromising the inner integrity of their calling. It is stressed by the Arabic historian, to whom Mr. Hodgson has drawn our attention. For the artist, who is concerned more with prestige than with his inner assignment, there is very real and strong pressure to yield up his integrity. This pressure is, in a sense, strongest in countries, like the majority of Latin American countries, where many artists feel that, for the sake of this prestige, they have to submit to the judgment of European and North American critics, if for no better reason than to reach the market. They feel that conformity will lead them to the big galleries, where they would like to see themselves hanging, as they actually sometimes hang but in another sense! This of course creates a very special atmosphere and produces what we might call cultural "Quislings", people who are willing to betray the very essence of their creative drive, in order to camouflage it in what are considered internationally respectable styles.

Here again I should avoid exaggerating the extent of such betrayals. The idiom of art is universal and one has every right – I would almost say one has an obligation – to be informed about the new styles. One should even appropriate from them what is convenient, provided one does not appropriate what is foreign to one's own creative effort. And this is where, of course, the greatness of the artist comes into play. The artist who is great is the one who can assimilate. The person of small talent falls into imitation. It is important to distinguish the one from the other.

This takes me finally to a suggestion of Mr. Hodgson's, when in his discussion of classics of other cultures, he proposed that a special academic title be conferred on those who made themselves proficient in at least two cultures. This is perhaps necessary for the man of letters, for persons who have to deal with the written word. In this connection I remember an incident in my life in connection with the great Spanish writer and scholar, Miguel Unamuno. I was terribly impressed once by the extraordinary scope of Unamuno's scholarship. He knew Sanskrit and Greek and Latin and Danish and Spanish. In this breadth of learning he was to a considerable extent characteristic of Spanish philosophers and Spanish culture, which by the way has not yet been mentioned in these discussions of ours. I was bewildered and baffled by the learning of this fellow Spaniard; then I had a sort of *satori* in the midst of my depression, which was caused by thinking how impossible it would be ever to match his phenomenal knowledge. Suddenly I came across an article by Unamuno where, in dealing with art, it was evident that he didn't have the smallest inkling of what Picasso was about. In other words, he was really rather blind to forms. He was blind to the culture of the eye. And then I realized, to my relief, that those of us who deal with the world of forms, with the world of the eye, in fact have a much greater, wider, way of understanding and of penetrating into the cultural world of other countries than those who have to confront the barrier of language. Here is a magnificent demonstration of the universality of the visual arts and of music.

So I would suggest to Mr. Hodgson not to restrict his proposed degree to those who achieve proficiency in two languages, [1] but to award it also to those who, by virtue of their mastery of a visual art or of music, speak in a language which is by its nature universal, and so speak as it were in all languages.

---

1. Squirru assumes that Hodgson does not, in his proposal, suggest awarding this *certificate* to a person who knows a classical tradition only through translations. There is no necessary conflict here with Grene's suggestion, for Grene was concerned, in making it, more with higher education in general than with graduate students who are specializing in the classics (ed.).

PART V: SPECIALIZATION AND GENERAL CULTURE

1. Reform of the Ecole des Mines at Nancy (France)

by

BERTRAND SCHWARTZ

A lot has been said about the training of engineers. It seems to me readily possible to agree on the aims of such training. Where discussion begins is about the means. In considering means it should be recognized that the true problem for the educator is to limit himself and to make a choice between different objectives; otherwise he will at best serve only knowledge, not intelligence, certainly not human understanding.

Our students at the *Ecole des Mines* in Nancy have already studied two or three years after taking the French Baccalaureate degree before arriving at our school. They then spend three years with us. There are 80 in a class. How were they trained before I came? How and why has the training been reformed?

Let me say right away that one of my objectives is to teach them how to use the knowledge they acquire. "Using" knowledge means to be able to "look for a problem, analyse it, acquire the necessary documentation, observe that, draw up a synthesis and communicate with others".

The most difficult and the most important matter is to recognize the important problems. I believe, indeed, that most of our engineers finally use very little of the knowledge they have acquired, because they have not learned how to link the different notions knowledge presents, or to relate them to everyday life.

When we, professors, deliver lectures, or draw up exercises for our students, we provide them, of course, with concrete examples, but we forget that these examples are artificially chosen, that they are removed from reality. As a matter of fact, if they were not, they would be very difficult to teach. The more we search for good pedagogic methods, the further our examples will be from everyday reality and the more difficult we shall make it for an engineer to utilize later on what he has learned at the school. Often, these engineers go home disgusted, because it is impossible for them to apply their knowledge in their profession.

Therefore, we are faced with a very serious problem: the link between the abstract and the concrete. I believe it is preferable to teach fewer subjects, but to teach our students how to relate these subjects to each other and to link them with reality. Otherwise their knowledge, though sometimes encyclopaedic, will be practicably inapplicable.

In view of what I have just said, you may take me for a utilitarian, a man who kills culture. As a matter of fact, I believe that knowledge becomes culture only if it is linked to the effective life. The important thing is to use what we have learned. In doing so, we automatically become aware of the need for learning new subjects. This is the real dynamic of education: the discovery for ourselves of fresh issues relevant to the individual purpose which takes form as our work proceeds.

What of communication? To communicate means to give as well as to receive from others. How does this generalization relate to the career of an engineer? In order to answer we need to speak a bit of what an engineer should not be and what he should be.

First he should not be an element in a very strict hierarchy. Nor does he need to master everything that his subordinates can do and understand. On the contrary, he works with a team as a kind of orchestra conductor. He must delegate his authority, instruct others, and think over his problems. And this involves reconsidering daily the organization he directs, and breaking new ground by applied research. Consequently he must learn not only scientific subjects, but also master relevant matters in economics and the social sciences.

I have found that, in order for an engineer to be creative and imaginative, we must encourage him to develop two specific qualities: uncommitted accessibility and independence. He must learn to stand aside from the engineering routine sufficiently to discern what is good or beautiful in anything new, to discover such qualities in an unknown individual. He must stand aside in order to avoid every rigid attitude.

At the same time he has to be independent in working. While he has to do with others as part of a team, he needs to form his own judgments as he works with them in order to understand what help and direction individuals among his group require. Professor Stone suggested at the end of his opening paper [1] that in order to understand others, one should first understand oneself. But in order to achieve this self-understanding, one

1. See above, p. 9.

must listen to others, which one can do must fruitfully by retaining one's intellectual and emotional independence, along with one's accessibility.

So much for my objectives.

In many ways, the old system of schooling in the *Ecole des Mines* stood in the way of achieving them. The emphasis was all on cramming knowledge down the students' throats. Too many subjects were taught: twenty new ones each year, sixty in three years. This left no time to assimilate what was learned, and no time during which our students could work on their own. Scientific subjects alone were taught; there was no study of economics or political science. The students listened to lectures, and were given no opportunity to participate in the subjects they studied. The insistence on traditional examinations increased their dependance on the professor and made it difficult for them to acquire any initiative.

How did the new system which I introduced improve this situation?

We set about, first, to reform the content and then the method of teaching.

Insofar as the curriculum was concerned we reduced the subjects taught from sixty to fifteen; five each year. Henceforth only one subject was taught each day, in order to give the student an opportunity to concentrate upon it. Concentration seems to me to be at the heart of general culture. We proceeded on the principle that one cannot know everything, that superficiality is the enemy of culture.

I come now to the method. As a matter of fact, real reform is an endless dynamic in which changes in methods involve changes in curriculum and vice versa. So the separation between content and methods that I am making in this description is for the sake of exposition only.

In connection with method, the students have now each day a period of instruction which lasts from three to three and a half hours. The rest of the day they are left free to work on their own. There are no lecture courses. There are no examinations.

How then do we proceed? How do we check up on a student's work?

Each day the students come after having prepared for themselves a new chapter of their course. The professor asks them to bring up for clarification any matters they have not understood. He answers their questions. This session lasts about twenty minutes at the most; and may be entirely suppressed if there are no questions.

The professor then gives a short lecture which does not exceed twenty minutes. He treats only the essentials of the subject. The students have to amplify his exposition with the help of documents (mimeographed papers, for the first year, books in French, English or German for the second and third years).

After these two twenty-minute periods, the students break up into small groups, each of fifteen, under the direction of assistants, for a stretch of work lasting about two hours. Two types of tests are made: control tests and self-appraisal tests. If the control test shows that a student has not done his work, he is automatically re-examined the following week on the matters in which he was deficient. This is the only way we have of making sure our students are doing their work regularly. Those who have not studied enough are given examinations at the end of the year as a sanction. Actually about one student out of the fifteen, on the average, has to take an examination. If he fails, he is called before a counsel of professors, and may be dismissed.

Now let me describe the self-appraisal tests. These are written and anonymous. The purpose is not to find out how a particular student works; but rather to enable the professor to determine how far the students generally have assimilated the material they are studying. The professor picks up the written papers which are submitted, corrects them and returns them, so that each student can measure his own progress and see how he stands in relation to the group as a whole.

This is a very important exercise for the instructor. Only in this way can he discover whether the students, as individuals, have understood the subject. Indeed, we always have the often erroneous feeling that our students are understanding what we say. Too often we ask: does everybody agree? Did everyone understand? And everybody seems to answer, yes! Nevertheless sometimes they have understood nothing! The self-appraisal tests provide us with a means of checking up on their and our understanding.

Self appraisal is also important for the students. It was suggested in one of the earlier meetings of this conference "Towards World Community" that experience often emerges from our *bad* judgment.[1] In order to be conscious of what we do *not* understand, we must already understand! The more we know, the more we test our ignorance.

Self appraisal helps to create this awareness. And it is most important for the students to sense that their teacher is also re-appraising his own attitude and work, in relation to them and to the subjects they are considering with him.

Who are these assistants who manage the tests, who instruct our students

1. See above, p. 33.

in these small groups? For all scientific work they are selected from the faculty of the University of Nancy. For all the rest (social science included) they are engineers employed in nearby industries. Each week about sixty engineers come from enterprises all around Nancy to partake in active instruction. I am convinced that this labor is very profitable to them, for, although their participation is voluntary, during the ten years that I have been in charge of this school I have never had any difficulty in getting the assistants I selected to serve.

Let us now return to the fifteen subjects that are taught. Formerly the subjects were all scientific. Now fifty percent of the curriculum is devoted to other subjects than science and technology.

Before going on to describe the other half of the curriculum, it is important to explain that in each of the three years the students are with us, they quit the classroom altogether for three-month periods to work in industry. During the first year they serve as manual workers, alongside regular manual workers, and they live with these workers' families. During the second year, they serve as technicians or foremen; during the third year, as engineers.

At each of these "stages", as we call them, their training is not merely technical. The object is to introduce our students to life – into the total life of those with whom they are to work. Through this practical training, they become aware that in the actual world they have eventually to enter, life is led under different conditions from the somewhat unreal ones at the school.

These three-month periods of industrial work are carefully prepared in advance, through the contacts that the school has with the presidents of particular enterprises. Each of the three periods of active work is immediately followed by a week-long seminar in which the students compare their experiences. The object of these seminars is to show how the particular experiences of individuals differ and that social problems are unlike mathematical or scientific problems: that there is no single answer to them.

The seminars are of the first importance in straightening out the ideas the students hold, which are often quite wrong. The seminar discussions help them to grasp the social problems they encounter as wholes.

I return now to the non-scientific curriculum in which students are trained as a part of their regular work at the school itself. This includes general economic theory, accounting, language courses, organization of work, psychology, sociology, and training in expression.

Psychology and sociology are taught, not only as part of the regular three-year curriculum during forty of the three-hour periods. They are also treated as part of the week-long seminars that follow each of the three stages of active industrial work. This is a further means of integrating theoretical training with practical experience.

The training in expression is divided into four parts. First, students are taught how to present in writing a report from given information (books or magazine articles, some of them technical). Secondly, they are trained in oral expression. They learn to listen to others, to modify their views in the light of what the others say, and to speak in public. This is a kind of course in dramatics designed to develop the sensibility of the participants. Thirdly, the students are taught how to carry out enquiries into particular problems and how to conduct surveys of particular subjects. Fourthly, they are taught to preside over and direct discussions.

It may be of interest, in concluding, to explain something of my own part in developing these reforms in the training of engineers. When I started I had in mind nothing beyond a better engineering training for the students, which would increase their knowledge of engineering, help them to assimilate it and to express themselves in the light of what they learned and assimilated. It was this objective that led me to cut down by at least half the period of formal instruction, and to reduce still more radically the number of subjects studied.

Later, in the process of directing the school, I came to realize that culture means "sharing". In order to share one's knowledge with others, one has to put oneself in their place. Out of that personal discovery emerged a new series of much more important, though less spectacular reforms.

Finally, I came to understand how, in order to encourage original outlooks among the students, it is necessary to evolve oneself both as a person and a teacher. For example, one has constantly to question one's ideas and outlook in order to encourage others to do the same. In order to achieve that end there was no need to change the organization of the school. But the spirit in which instruction was carried on had to change radically.

When I began my reforms, I had not understood their many implications. And even now I am not sure I have entirely mastered these implications. Perhaps doubt is a part of the educational process for the teacher. In any event the future of the reforms may help to determine whether or not my effort has been utopian!

2. International Commerce as a School for Understanding

by

WILLIAM WOOD PRINCE

In discussing Mr. Schwartz's paper, I should like to keep in mind Mr. Nef's remarks about the creative role that commerce has played in culture.[1] I think we should realize it is not only the visual arts, or music, or literature that can contribute to international understanding, but also business itself. Business shares many of the aspects of art. Particularly today, as we all know, as business institutions become more complex, they need to be organized. Organizing matters of business resembles organizing the materials of a work of art. We business men are faced with the same old struggle as the artist, between form and content.

So I am delighted by Bertrand Schwartz's concepts for educating engineers. The initiative he has described should greatly aid in our problem, as businessmen, of bringing together subject matter and form. In a business organization, people are the subject matter. The form is represented by the lines of communication, the orders for goods and the directions to the staff.

As I see it, we are facing today a period where engineers and scientists must and will play a more important part than ever before in the conduct of business. Yet, I am sorry to say, it is rare indeed that we find a person, trained in engineering or in science, who is capable of directing business enterprise. There are, of course, many notable exceptions. But, by and large, the education conventionally received by engineers and scientists does not present us with persons skilled in communication, skilled in the persuasive powers which are necessary, or skilled as negotiators in commercial transactions.

I recall one time flying to Europe, to negotiate a contract, when I had

---

1. Nef, *United States and Civilization*, Chicago 1967, pp. 395–402, esp. pp. 400–401.

with me an outstanding engineer of our firm. In discussing our objective with him, I said, "Well, we might give a little here, and so forth, but on one point we must stand firm." He said, "Well, don't worry about that. I have my slide rule with me, and I can prove that point any time!" Unfortunately, negotiations do not go by the slide rule.

It will be hard for you to realize that even in a lowly packing company like ours,[1] our sausage formulas are made by computers. But this is the type of world we now live in. So it is necessary to entrust more and more of our discussions, in part, to engineers and scientists. It is important, therefore, to educate them to be more than "slide-rule" judges. Bertrand Schwartz has emphasized this and I am sorry he did not pursue the matter farther. I would like to know more concretely how the other fifty percent of the study time is spent at his school, the time devoted to subjects other than science and technology. He spoke of the practical experience the students get in industry, but are they being given courses in the humanities, in literature and art, so they may become more rounded people? I think such courses are essential.[2]

As scientists and engineers become more important in the conduct of our affairs, they will come across one of the main problems which confronts all business leaders. How to motivate people. I don't like the phrase. Nevertheless we do need leaders in business willing and eager to achieve goals towards which science and technology are powerless to guide them.

I assume that the goals they seek will depend a good deal upon their education. It may be sterilizing if, in engineering schools, you devote the time of study just to mathematics, statistics and engineering, even if this is combined with the management of men and the social problems this management presents. Then when one does come out into life and into a position in industry or government or commerce, the areas of interest or areas of motivation are limited, in the wrong way, in a sterilizing way. If they are so limited, it is hard to see how the scientists and engineers can grasp effectively the nature of the part that industries ought to take in the whole new social structure the world presents today.

I would like to leave a last thought. We are being led today into a much more closely woven structure of government, education, business and indeed world affairs. All these fields are even more interdependent, more interrelated. Maybe some of our governments do not like giant corporations, but it is giant corporations that can, properly guided and properly

1. Mr. Prince is Chairman of the Board of Armour and Company.
2. Mr. Schwartz explained that no regular courses are given at his school in the arts or in literature.

controlled, lead towards a greater understanding of the world community we are seeking to serve by this conference.

It is a concept today of most large businesses that, when they embark on a new venture, either in the United States or overseas, they employ foreign capital invested with us, in this country, and also invest capital in other countries. So in these joint ventures overseas you have foreign partners, whether they be French or German or Japanese or Argentine. It is the same in the United States. Here too you have foreign partners whether they be German, French, Argentine, Japanese. They all become part of one corporation. So you find you have to sit down, you have to reach an organizational understanding on an international basis. Such an organizational understanding, I think, underlies the whole structure of our today's civilization. If wisely conceived, it can lead towards the goals for which John Nef has worked consistently during at least the last quarter century.

3. Insurance and Culture

by

HERMON DUNLAP SMITH

I should like to make a few comments about Mr. Schwartz's paper of a general nature, and then make a few observations based on my experience.

First of all, on the point that Mr. Prince made, about the importance of a broad education, I want to emphasize that, as he suggested, this has become far more important than it ever was before, from the industrial point of view. We have many more instances of engineers who are arriving at top managerial posts. That is because of the increasing relevance of the whole subject of engineering to business.

While the need for broadening the education of engineers has been increasingly recognized, the difficulty of providing for this need is great. More is expected of engineers, and so much more technical instruction has to be given than was once the case. Hence there is constant pressure to squeeze out the little time left for cultural and humanistic work.

Certain of the engineering schools in the United States have recently made a very concentrated effort to broaden their curriculum. This is particularly true of the Massachusetts Institute of Technology. The same tendency to leave room for a broader training is also becoming apparent in certain law schools. This is certainly true of the Yale Law School, which in fact has been criticized on the ground that it does not teach enough law, that it is too much concerned with general culture. The University of Chicago Law School has taken steps also towards a broader training.

My own business experience is in the field of insurance.[1] Insurance is not quite a profession. One hardly thinks of it in terms of a discipline requiring a highly specialized graduate training, such as is essential in medicine, and to a certain degree in law. In insurance you need some technical training

1. Mr. Smith was President of Marsh & McLennan, Inc.

but not the degree of it that, at a graduate level certainly, would to my mind qualify it as a profession.

This raises the whole question whether business is a profession, in the sense that it requires a specific professional training. I think there has almost been a tendency to overemphasize the need for professional training in business. In our insurance business, which is perhaps typical of insurance generally and even of business generally, I think we would prefer a broadly based, intelligent young man who has pursued studies in the humanities, maybe in English literature, maybe in Greek philosophy. This is in fact the policy which we have followed in my firm. We take a man humanistically trained right out of college, bring him into the office, let him get his technical training at a night school somewhere. We welcome him on the theory that, once he has had this kind of humanistic start, he will continue his broader education by general reading. We think that he will grow into a more competent and more valuable leader in our business than someone who has devoted his preliminary training to worrying about the operation of the insurance business, someone who comes to us as a competent insurance man. Business needs men of the world. I have felt that humanistic training is more valuable than too much emphasis on the technical. And while insurance is different from engineering and from medicine, when engineers (and I believe physicians too) are called to administer business enterprises, as Mr. Prince's account of his experience with one of them has suggested, what they need above all is the imaginative approach which a broad liberal education ought to stimulate.

4. Cultural Possibilities in Specialized Curricula

HAROLD ROSENBERG

I am very much interested in Mr. Schwartz's paper, because in teaching painting in art schools or in universities, there exists a problem comparable to his in training engineers. I am not talking about teaching art *history*. I am talking about what they call "studio courses," where the objective is to turn out painters.

This is a new situation, one that has developed enormously since the war. Artists used to learn in other artists' studios. But there has been an enormous drive in the last ten years to teach art in the universities. And the question always comes up, to what degree students can pursue professional training for the practice of an art, while being pulled in all directions by the humanities courses they are required to take in order to get a bachelor's degree. There have been many different approaches to this problem. Usually the studio major, although he presumably devotes most of his time to learning how to paint and draw, is actually diverted by his other studies and complains that he cannot concentrate sufficiently on his main task. Mr. Schwartz's success in getting engineering students to spend half their time on other subjects than engineering contrasts with the difficulties encountered in getting art students to turn aside from painting and drawing. This contrast might suggest that an engineer who studies only engineering is likely to become a barbarian more readily than a painter who studies only painting and drawing!

But is there really so great a difference? And is the remedy for the student-engineer or the student-artist to be found only in the reallotment of time which Mr. Schwartz has described?

In almost any subject, whether it is engineering or transportation or painting, one has a center of human culture in the subject itself. By studying the history of engineering, one is, in an important sense, studying the whole history of mankind, because mankind became mankind when humans started to engineer things and stuff instead of just running around from tree to tree. The same thing is true about, let's say, meat packing, or any other subject. Once it becomes a subject of study, that is, if it becomes self conscious, then it already becomes the potential center out of which to move towards other kinds of knowledge. For example, law is of course nothing but a formulation of various historical events and various changes in the power structure of states, so that the law student doesn't need to study history the way, let's say, a student of biology might also need to know something about history. The law student might very well study history in terms of the evolution of law. And in art there's no subject that hasn't in one way or another impinged upon painting or poetry.

Plato discusses this in one of his dialogues. He raises the question as to whether Homer really had any experience with boat building, since he seems to describe the building of ships as if he possessed technical knowledge of that craft. Homer seems to know what he sings about. But since Plato concluded that Homer couldn't have had any first hand knowledge of such a subject, he decided that Homer must have been inspired by the gods. Which is a nice way to get out of it!

The fact of the matter is that anyone studying literature or painting or engineering, or, let us say, boatbuilding, becomes at once involved in the whole of the humanities, but from a point of view that is much more vital than that of the student who is merely handed the menu, that is, the usual academic catalogue. Yet, we neglect this fact and either give the student the humanities at the expense of his art training, so that he won't come out of college looking as if he had merely studied carpentry, so that he will appear to be a cultivated person, even though he is only an artist. Or we let him study art and let his education in the humanities go to the devil – let him shift for himself when it comes to that. Neither of these courses is really satisfactory. So I think the future may well lie in building the curricula around specialities, which, imaginatively understood, can be seen as part of culture as a whole.

I offer this only as an experimental idea.[1]

1. See below, p. 117, note.

RAFAEL SQUIRRU

I think it is a very good idea. But it presents a problem. In the time of the Renaissance, the fact that you were a painter meant that you were a kind of chemist and that you were investigating a whole series of interrelated subjects that arose out of your calling. Now, instead you go to a store and you buy your paints and all your materials.

So it would not be a bad thing if the artist were encouraged once more to become also a craftsman in the Renaissance sense. This would automatically introduce him into the field of science and technology, and I for one am not comfortable with the idea of complete separation. As Mr. Rosenberg suggested, people today tend to think of the barbarism of the scientist or technocrat because he doesn't have the humanities, but they forget the complementary barbarity. This is very prevalent, I'm afraid, among those today who specialize in the arts to the point of forgetting the rest of life. In order to become truly human it is necessary to be a whole human being. It seems to me that art today has tended to become less complete than it was when artists had to take care of those technical problems of their materials themselves. So I would add to Mr. Rosenberg's most valid plea for a new kind of specialization the suggestion that artists should be encouraged to experiment with their own tools.

MARSHALL G. S. HODGSON

I am repeatedly drawn to the feeling that the curricular problem as such (that concerns us in this discussion) is essentially insoluble. In a sense Mr. Rosenberg has given us as good a solution as is possible, in terms of building from a center represented by training for a special calling.[1] Yet I wonder whether we may not still be laying our stress on an ideal or pattern *curri-*

---

1. This was the idea in my mind, based on my experience as an economic historian, when I founded twenty-six years ago the first entirely interdisciplinary faculty in any university, The Committee on Social Thought: the idea that a new kind of concentration upon a special subject of research should lead the student into the whole of culture. Some of the results in the case of individuals, for example the late Marshall Hodgson, have been most satisfactory, and institutes similar to the Committee on Social Thought, of which he was Chairman, could do much to arrive at the kind of training encouraged by Messrs. Rosenberg, Squirru and Hodgson (ed.).

culum to the neglect of the individual human being and his training. We tend to forget that, in spite of all we can criticize in any existing curriculum, good education does manage to happen. Oddly enough, one person may be very well educated in the same class where another person is not at all well educated. This is the point I should like to start from.

As has been many times said, each student needs to build his own education, and each teacher needs to build his own way of educating. And we have got to mesh the two together, so that the right students find the right teachers. There's no use telling a teacher who uses one kind of method that he'd better use some other, unless he is temperamentally and in other ways prepared for it. And I'm quite convinced that some teachers, for instance, can do a marvellous job of teaching by way of extremely authoritarian discipline, even though by and large we say this is no longer what is required in education. As a matter of fact, some people who have done a wonderful job of teaching have done it that way. I think we should allow for that possibility.

The problem that arises when we let professors and students loose to find one another, each in terms of his own center of interest and what seem to be in each case his greatest possibilities, is the problem of maintaining standards. This social-cultural problem is terribly visible. If one compares, for instance, the development of education in certain societies with certain others, one becomes aware of the value of some of the restrictive guidelines "You must know this" and "You must know that"; "You must teach this way" and "You must teach that way." These orders have a very real purpose.

If we neglect the problem of maintaining standards, we may contribute to a real lowering of the awareness, or the relative awareness, and the competence of the whole population. What I should like to see, then, is a thrust (a further thrust, because I think we are already moving in this direction) toward developing a much more multiple and flexible basis for maintaining standards. Actually, the specialized department at a university which insists that its students study this and that and the other thing, is not the only means now at our disposal for maintaining standards. We have professional societies; we have government boards that test competencies; we have editors of professional journals; we have various private organizations. All of these help to maintain standards in various ways.

I would like to see the pattern developed in which maintenance of standards was increasingly the function of a variety of different independent bodies. Then the university, even though it still might give a bachelor's degree for its own students on the basis of its own curriculum, would not be tied to this, for there would be other certificates, other norms available to the student besides those established by his own university. You might then find a student coming to the University of Chicago and not aiming to get a Chicago degree but to prepare himself for a certificate to be given by some private board, testifying that he has a certain kind of cultural competence and that the board has duly tested and examined his credentials, which might be quite independent from the specific training he had at the university. (Of course, such certificates should be multiple, so that any one of them was clearly optional – otherwise the student's flexibility might be reduced rather than enhanced.)

To tie this in, as I am disposed to do, with Professor Hayek's idea of "a self-generating order" is perhaps somewhat forced. I should not quite call myself a liberal in Mr. Hayek's sense anyhow. I make the association because it seems to me that the building up of structures at a fairly abstract level for developing standards, removed from the actual instruction, would make for flexibility in the academic curriculum. There could be greater freedom within the university, because of an order generated independently. The independent boards could make possible competition for different sorts of certificates, unrelated to the local academic community, and based on the kind of prestige they would have in terms of the kind of people, the quality of the people, who were seeking and attaining these certificates.

Such a development might solve many of our present problems of curriculum. Now the faculties of a university lay down positive norms for what the student must learn, only to find they would have to prescribe for study, in order to meet these norms, ten times as much as a person can possibly learn. If the students and professors were allowed to choose each other more freely, the whole problem of developing curricula might be moved into a realm with far more universal possibilities, for each individual would have to discover his own cultural synthesis and raise it to a level where it could find independent validation. The institutions that offer the education would no longer have to designate exactly what the result of an education must be, and to testify that a student had fulfilled the requirements; such functions could be left to an open cultural market place. Of course, far more intensive personal guidance and advising would have to be done in the universities; but we are rapidly learning how to offer just that, and presumably relief from other administrative duties could release energies – both among faculty and among older students – to that end.

It is my impression that we are developing increasingly other scholarly standards than just the one connected with a particular institution. Students now may very well be getting their education at such an institution, with a purpose formed outside and independently of it, a purpose which may even be in conflict with the purposes that are governing that institution. The more the high standards we should insist upon are maintained in multiple independent places – partly through the government, partly through private individual associations – the freer both the student and the professor will be, within a university, to formulate the educational possibilities important to both in terms of the special talents of the professor and in terms of the special needs of the student.

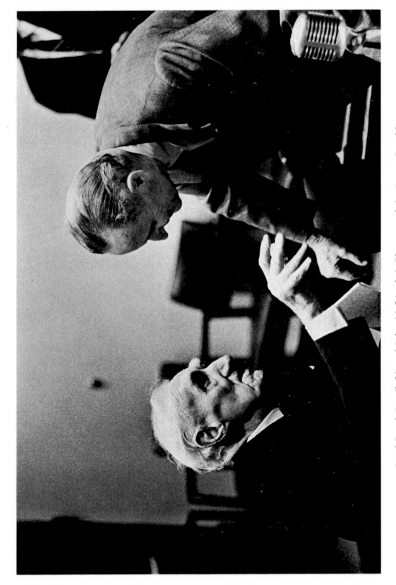

Lord Boyd Orr (left) and John Nef (right). Photograph by James Stricklin.

PART VI: ABOVE ALL NATIONS IS HUMANITY

1. A Breakthrough?

by

Lord Boyd Orr

When I was invited to attend this Conference my first thought was to re-fuse as it would not be worth the trouble of coming such a long distance to another International Conference. I have attended these in most coun-tries, from Japan to the United States, and find that though all reach the same general conclusions that measures should be taken to avoid war and to eliminate distressing poverty in the world, when the recommendations are submitted to the United Nations and to governments no action follows and I thought this might be another Conference of the same kind. How-ever, when I read the letter from Professor Nef, your Chairman, I thought this Conference might be the beginning of a breakthrough in the present cold war.

Education and a better understanding between nations might lead nations, at present in conflict, each to consider the position of what they regarded as an enemy country – the reason for their fear and hate – and to consider also what measures they might agree upon as beneficial to both. As Mr. Truman, your former President, said "If Russia and America could agree upon a world policy on agriculture which would be beneficial to both it would be easier to solve their political differences". So I came to this Conference with a vision, which may have been a mirage, of the principal countries setting up Centers for Human Understanding like this which might be a means of getting people in the world to understand what all the trouble was about and what measures might be taken to achieve what all sensible people want, a world free from war and poverty.

I cannot tell you anything you do not know already. The only contri-bution I can make is to speak of my limited vision of the world today from my training as a scientist and a business man. In my opinion the world to-day is suffering from the terrific impact of modern science. Increase in knowledge, which gives man more powers over his environment and creates new ideas and ideals, brings about confusion and conflict until society has been adjusted so that the new powers and new ideas can be adapted to peaceful ends.

Such confusion and conflict always occurs. For many thousands of years before the setting up of settled communities human society consisted of relatively small groups with flocks and herds wandering to find grazing grounds and roots and primitive grains to replace the fruits and nuts of their tree-dwelling ancestors. The roving herdsmen who in times of drought had been accustomed to coming down to the well-watered river basins, where the settlements had taken place, now found them occupied, with the result that fighting broke out between the food producers and the food gatherers as is illustrated in the Bible in the story of Cain the cultivator and Abel the herdsman.

So it has been all through history. For instance, after the Renaissance, when man gained freedom of thought and freedom of speech which had been denied in the thousand years of the Dark Ages, there was a conflict between the orthodox people who wanted no change and the more enlightened people who wanted change. This ended in the terrible Thirty Years War in Europe.

In England where kings had been accustomed to rule by Divine Right the rising merchant and industrial middle class rebelled against that old idea. This resulted in a civil war with the unheard of execution of a king and the setting up of a temporary republic.

In Britain during the Industrial Revolution of the nineteenth century, when the peasants had been driven off the land to become workers in the industrial towns and had a lower standard of living than they had had as peasants, the Chartist movement began with the people marching and shouting "Bread or Blood". This led to the abolition of the Corn Laws, cheaper food and a rapid rise in the standard of living of the common people. This was a time when Karl Marx wrote his *Capital* when it looked as if the people of the world were becoming poorer and poorer and the wealthy wealthier. As a matter of fact it did not turn out like that in Britain where the poor have become richer and the rich poorer.

In the last few decades, during the lifetime of people of my age, science has made enormous advances and given man tremendous new powers. They are now able to release nuclear energy. They can make bombs, one of which of 50 megatons could completely destroy buildings and kill about ten million people if dropped on a city like London or New York. There is the equivalent of ten tons of T.N.T. for every man, woman and child in the world today. It is possible for a war with these weapons to destroy our civilisation. In addition to the Hydrogen Bomb there are new biological weapons of war. Dr. Brock Chisholm, who was a major general in charge of germ warfare to be used if the Germans did so in the last war, said at a meeting in the Waldorf Astoria Hotel in New York that the atom bomb could kill fewer people than the new disease-causing germs. These would destroy people the way myxomatosis destroyed ninety per cent of the rabbits in Britain and Australia.

On the other hand, the same science which has produced these terrible instruments of death could be used to eliminate poverty, hunger and preventable disease. Already in the wealthy nations, able to employ the necessary measures, the average expectation of life of children born at the present day has been increased to seventy years whereas in the 1870s it was only forty years. The gift of thirty years of life on an average for every child born today is as important for the common people of the world as putting a man on the moon, on which we are spending so much money.

Fifty or sixty years ago it was impossible to provide sufficient food for all the people in the world because the population always tended to increase faster than the power to produce food. Today, with modern technology, it is possible to provide food, clothing, housing and all the physical necessities for a full life for every man, woman and child in the world. I remember reading a book with a Foreword by Mrs. Eleanor Roosevelt in which some economists or industrialists estimated that, if modern technology were applied to the things men need instead of to war, it would be possible for a man with only seven years' work to provide sufficient wealth, but without luxury, for himself and his family for the whole of his lifetime. That may have been an exaggeration, but it is an indication of the enormous powers of technology to produce wealth. The difficulty in the present age is not to produce the wealth but to get it distributed to prevent the slowing down of industries and the spread of unemployment.

So it is that today we have, on the one hand, the possibility of war with death and destruction which could make the human race join the long list of species which have become extinct because they could not become adjusted to new conditions, or, on the other hand, by applying these new powers to peaceful ends, we could have a higher condition of physical welfare and culture for all the people of the world than has ever been enjoyed by the most privileged people in the most privileged nations. *The decision is literally a matter of life or death.*

There is another great change which modern science has brought about. In the 1870s, before the telephone appeared, the quickest way of sending messages beyond the range of the human voice was by carrier pigeon, flag waving or reflection of sunlight by mirrors. Today it is physically possible for a man addressing an audience in a hall to be heard by people in nearly every country in the world as soon as by the people in the hall. Even more remarkable, it is possible for people to see, on television screens, events taking place thousands of miles away.

Fifty years ago it took about three weeks to come from India to England. Today with the jet plane one can dine in Bombay and have breakfast in London next morning. This has created entirely new conditions in the world. In the old days a nation could have an independent policy. Today the world is so small that the affairs and interests of nations are so interdependent that it is impossible for any great event to take place in any part of the world without all nations being directly or indirectly involved. As Wendell Wilkie said, "We are now one world". It is equally true to say that all nations in the world which have become a common community will ultimately share the same fate.

The settlement of differences between any two nations can only be achieved at an international level involving the consent of all nations. The people of the world recognise this. For example, the game of Association Football used to be limited to games played by local or national teams. Today the teams ignore all political boundaries. Teams from Great Britain have been playing Poland, France has been playing Spain. At the Boat Race on the Thames the Russians send a boat to compete. When they win they are cheered by the whole crowd because the crowd recognises that they are sportsmen. Now the people of the world are getting together in sport in the Olympic Games. So far as sport is concerned we have become one world by agreement.

And so it is with business. Jefferson, the great President of the United States, said that business men recognise no political boundaries. Wherever they can trade and make a profit there they are, and there they are today doing just that. In spite of all the political boundaries they are surmounting them. Thousands of merchants of Western Europe are going to Russia and China buying and selling. In Moscow a few years ago there was a great British Fair. I attended it hoping to get orders for Scotland. I found that the Western technicians and the Russian technical bureaucrats were discussing precision instruments and types of steel and so on, and deciding which British products would suit the Russian markets and which Russian products would suit the British markets. One Conservative member of the British government was present and I asked him how he had been able to go to Russia when the government was against trading in many kinds of goods with Russia. He said "I went to Winston Churchill and explained that we were going to try to get orders. Churchill said 'Go, certainly – the more trade the better'".

The British business men and the Russian technicians could agree because they defined their terms and so they knew what they were talking about. They got together as scientists do. It is interesting that at the Moscow Fair I was staying at the Ukraine Hotel and saw a group of about a dozen men at a special table. I am a member of the New York Academy of Science and saw an American Fellow of the Academy at this table so I went across and said, "What are you boys doing here? This is a Trade Fair." He replied, "We are engaged in research on cancer and we have come across to discuss it with our Russian colleagues engaged in the same research." They had no thought of political differences. For them science had no boundaries. Scientists the world over define their terms and can understand each other and are keen to co-operate.

Another thing which has struck me forcibly is that governments recognise that we are now one world and in their propaganda they appeal not only to their own people but to the people of the whole world. Almost every day I receive a propaganda document from a foreign government which I suppose goes to every member of Parliament. They come from Russia, China, North Vietnam, Korea, South Africa, Cyprus. They are all appealing for support from worldwide public opinion. Governments are beginning to realise this and are coalescing into groups like N.A.T.O., C.E.A.T.O., the Warsaw Group and so on. But these are unstable groupings. Yugoslavia has broken away. Romania now makes trade agreements with Poland. Even Britain is now making trade agreements with Communist countries. The only logical outcome is not a series of groups but one group, a world community with a central government which can consider measures beneficial for the people of all countries.

What are the obstacles to this desirable end? The first is the ideological conflict between Capitalism and Communism. This could be got over if politicians would define their terms as scientists and business men do. Communism is an impossible economic system under which there could be no further progress. It is impossible, with human nature as it is, for everybody to agree to put all their wealth into a common pool. You may remember that it was tried in the early Christian Church when Ananias and Sapphira, who were land owners, kept back a part of their land for themselves. They wished to be a bit better than their neighbours. They had a sad fate. They were carried out dead and buried by the young men.

What politicians mean by Communism today is the system in Russia under which the government controls all industry and distribution and under which a Leader is built up as a Superman. His word is law and he has the power to imprison any person who offers criticism. We had this form of Communism in Britain during both world wars. Members of Parliament or others who criticised the government were put in prison and Lloyd George in the first world war and Churchill in the second were built up as Supermen. In the last war it was impossible for a farm worker to leave one farm and be exchanged for a worker on another farm even though both the farmers and the men wished the change. Under the emergencies of war this was necessary to get a unified national effort. It was the same in Russia when Stalin was mobilising all his labour to produce weapons to resist an invasion from the west, which he feared and which actually happened. He, however, was more ruthless than the British. People who tried to criticise were killed.

In Britain, when the war was won, conditions were immediately relaxed and people who had been imprisoned were set free, and I think every one of them was given honours. One was raised to the House of Lords, and many others got knighthoods or other honours. In Russia today, when it has become a great world power, there is increasing freedom of speech and they are now beginning to adopt the profit motive as being better for production than the totalitarian detailed control of industry.

China is a Communist country. When Mao took over in 1949 he did not introduce Communism. He confiscated the land of the war lords and gave it to the peasants, but he allowed the wealthy to keep their wealth. He took partial control of industry but left the old managers to run the industries and make as much profit as they could. In discussion with one of the head men of the Chinese Bank we estimated that there were more millionaires in China than in England. In 1959, the last time I was there, when everything in China was flourishing, Mao said "Let every flower flourish and every school of thought contend." He thought the time had come to relax the vigorous government control. Since then the surrounding of China with bombing bases and the invasion of Vietnam has made the Chinese fear that they would be invaded again as they had been for the last 150 years and the complete totalitarian system would be re-introduced.

I am not afraid of Communism. It may be necessary in an emergency, but where you have an educated people so soon as the emergency is past they demand to have freedom restored because freedom of thought and speech is the most essential freedom. In Britain after the first world war Lloyd George, who had been the great man, was voted out of office, and

Churchill, to his astonishment, at the first General Election after the second world war, was driven from office. So soon as it had been made plain that the freedom-loving people of Britain would not tolerate a Superman in time of peace, they voted him back into power five years later. The important thing in the world today is education to enable people to think for themselves and to value freedom of thought and speech.

Another obstacle is the revolt of the coloured races. The white European race, of which America is an off-shoot, dominated the whole world from the sixteenth to the nineteenth centuries by military or economic power, and there is no doubt that they exploited the countries of the coloured people. Now, with education, radio and the cinematograph these people begin to understand things. They blame their poverty on the exploitation of the white races and are in revolt. They no longer tolerate being treated as inferior people. Travelling in Asia I have often heard Asians say "They dropped the bomb on Hiroshima because we are coloured. They did not drop it on the Germans because they are white". It does not matter if this is not true. They believe it, and it motivates their actions. In my opinion, having visited Russia and China many times, the present difficulties between these two Communist countries are caused by the fact that the Chinese think the Russians are white and that they will go with America which they say they admire.

The white races have got to learn that they are not innately superior to people who have a different colour of skin. Coloured men, two of them negroes, have received many Nobel Prizes. Some years ago a negro from Ghana won the prize as the most distinguished and brilliant medical student at Glasgow University where there are about 1,500 medical students, and Jomo Kenyatta has shown that they can be able administrators. He has brought about peace and co-operation between the coloured and the whites in Kenya.

One of the big adjustments which must be made to stop the revolt of the coloured people is to recognise them as human beings with equal rights with the white races and to raise their standard of living as rapidly as possible. Two-thirds of the people in the world, consisting mainly of coloured people, are so poor that thousands die from starvation and malnutrition. This is due to the fact that owing to the spread of preventive medicine the populations of the coloured countries are increasing more rapidly than their food supply in spite of all the work being done by F.A.O. and the excellent work of organisations like the Rockefeller and Ford Foundations.

The amount of food per head of the people in the world is actually decreasing.

Such is the position of the world as I see it today. The armaments race, if continued, will certainly lead to a war which would mean the end of our civilisation and the extinction of the human species. On the other hand we have the power to create a new era free from the intolerable evils of war, hunger and preventable disease. This can be brought about by a world government. This was tried in the League of Nations and very nearly succeeded. It was tried again in the United Nations, which has not fulfilled the hopes of the people of the world. The gap between the old world, with every nation having complete sovereignty, and the new world, where that is no longer possible, is difficult to close. I suggest we might follow Mr. Truman's idea of getting the nations to agree to co-operate on some business plan which would be of mutual advantage to all countries. Solving the world food and population problems would make an excellent beginning on the long march to world government. In the 1930s, when there was widespread unemployment and decreasing foreign trade, the League of Nations approved a Plan for a World Food Policy based on human needs. This would have led to the elimination of hunger in the world and a rise in the standard of living of the coloured races. As the world food supply would need to be nearly doubled to feed the present population, it would have led to an enormous demand for the industrial products such as fertilisers, agricultural implements, pumps for irrigation schemes, food containers and so on, and a great expansion of world trade. Committees were set up to work out the plan. Russia, America and Western European countries worked together on it and by 1938 the delegates from twenty-two governments with their financiers, scientists and industrialists were meeting in Conference to work out the plan in greater detail. This was brought to an end by the outbreak of war in 1939. Then America called the Hot Springs Conference in 1943 which revived the plan and from this arose F.A.O. But when the Director General of F.A.O. put forward an outline of the plan with the economic and political benefits which would accrue, it was approved by all the delegates to the Conference at Copenhagen in 1946 with the exception of the British delegate who wanted the whole scheme referred to the International Trade Organisation (which is now defunct). Britain's view was that her wealth had been built up by cheap imports of food, low wages and big profits, and the World Food Board might raise the price of wheat which was against the interests of Britain. Then, when the delegates of the main countries met in Washington six months later to work out the plan in more detail, America withdrew saying that the great powers, by which it meant Britain and America, were not prepared to give any funds or authority to any organisation for any such purpose even though Russia was prepared to join if Britain and America did.

Since then governments have learned more sense. The British Prime Minister put the establishment of a World Food Board on to his Election Program, and President Kennedy, with whom I had a long interview shortly before he was assassinated, went to the United Nations and said that America would support a World Food Policy that would give an adequate diet to every child in the world.

The difficulty is where the money is to come from. We are spending about 160 billion dollars on war and preparation for war. Governments say that they recognise the need for disarmament but cannot agree upon the method. I suggest that they could begin disarmament by every country in the world cutting its military budget by, say, 10 per cent, keeping half the saving to reduce taxation or for other needs, and devoting the other half to an international fund managed by business men to enable the food deficit countries to purchase, first food and then fertilisers and other things needed to increase production, on condition that the loans given for this purpose would begin to yield interest or be repaid so soon as hunger had been abolished.

The co-operation of nations on this plan would be beneficial to them all. The slowing down of industries producing weapons of war would be compensated for by producing the vast amount of industrial products needed to double world food production. The co-operation of the nations on a concrete plan, for the benefit of the people of the world and for economic prosperity, would be an important step to further co-operation for the application of the great powers of modern science to bring about a new age of peace and prosperity.

What is needed today is leadership. Governments, I am convinced, cannot give the necessary leadership. They are fully occupied with the day-to-day problems and in manoeuvering to win the next Election. The leadership must come from the people not interested in party politics, scientists, men of learning and from the people of the world who must be given a vision of the wonderful new age which we could hand over to our children if science were applied for the promotion of the welfare of all the people of the world. That new era, free from the terrible evils of war, poverty and hunger, is within our reach. The people of the world want it. Let us give them the leadership and human society will achieve it. That leadership can be brought about by the most intelligent people in the world meeting together for a better human understanding, finding out why nations hate and fear each other and how these fears could be abolished, seeing the great problems of the world today and offering tentative solutions. That is what Centers for Human Understanding could bring about if they were established in all the most powerful countries in the world.

2. Postlude: A Fresh Foreign Policy

by

JOHN NEF

" ... cette activité étrange qui a poussé et poussera tou-
jours les hommes à s'entretuer, quand un peu de charité
et moins d'avidité suffiraient à assurer la paix éternelle."

Guillaume Apollinaire, *La Femme assise*
(Paris, 1920), p. 187

The "strange exertion of energy" (as Apollinaire calls it) in mutual
slaughter – between tribes, later between states, and most recently between
vast coalitions of nations – has been until now a luxury the human race
could afford, because the violence worked itself out short of the virtually
total destruction of both sides. Then suddenly, within the lifetime of the
generations who fought two world wars, it became practicable to kill tens
of millions within a few hours. It became practicable to destroy more people
in a couple of days than the eighty million or so who died as a result of
organized fighting in the ten years 1914 to 1918 and 1939 to 1945.

Nor is that all. The unprecedented pulverization of life and property can
be effected before any of the excitement and enthusiasm – the glamor –
modern war has hitherto generated has even begun to wear off. Both
history [1] and psychology [2] suggest how much less gruesome and repellent
humans in modern itmes, since the seventeenth century, have found
killing and being killed impersonally, when neither the killers nor their
victims see the enemy, than when they have to resort to bloody bodily
combat. If the new weapons were unleashed, a kind of shroud would
envelop tens of millions as the blow struck and generations were ob-
literated.

War has ceased to be "bearable". War is "suicide"[3]. Can the hatred and

---

1. John Nef, *War and Human Progress*, Cambridge, Mass., 1950 (also in paperback by Norton,
New York, 1968) pp. 251 ff., 371–374, and passim.
2. Henri Bergson, *The Two Sources of Morality and Religion*, New York 1935, pp. 135–36.
3. Edwin Hubble, "The War That Must Not Happen" (1946), in *The Nature of Science and
Other Lectures*, San Marino, Calif. 1954, pp. 75–76.

violence, the power and the glory, the sadism and masochism, the lure of self-destruction, released under respectable auspices in the organized war that some humans through the centuries have found so exhilarating and so satisfying to their patriotism, discover less threatening outlets? Have men and women within them the humanity to muster the extra grains of compassion, to husband the additional restraints on their cupidity and their pride, that are now necessary to provide a future for the novel experiment in civilized improvement which began at least as early as the late sixteenth century?[1] Or will they drift into suicide? That should now become the basic question underlying the foreign policy of every nation.

The peace we might hope to salvage during the coming decades would not be total, let alone eternal. Even if organized war between nations should be eliminated before man's recent material conquests are liquidated, struggle, suffering and trouble will always abound. They are the ransom for living. The "deadly boring" conditions which Professor Devons says "most people" dread, would not be the price of peace. Utopia is no imminent threat[2] to the zest for life civilization has brought to many. The universal Hell, which thermo-nuclear engagements or the saturation of the atmosphere with deadly germs could produce, is.

The dialogue provided in these pages is part of the search a Center for Human Understanding has inaugurated for ways of ending that threat. The discussions show that the prevalence of "nationalism" in every country is a major barrier[3] to making effective the knowledge, the exchanges, the art and the kinds of education which are now working in the direction of world community. A reasonably peaceful planet, whereon most people would be delivered from the threat of sudden extinction, is not possible unless commitment to humanity supersedes, as the primary loyalty, commitment to one's nation. The "brotherhood of man" under "the fatherhood of God" would have to become more than a cliché.

The constraint at present imposed on persons in government service

1. Nef, *The Conquest of the Material World*, Chicago, 1964, pp. 142–43, 212, 219–21; Nef, *The United States and Civilization*, 2nd ed., Chicago, 1967, pp. 22–26; Eric Kerridge, *The Agricultural Revolution*, London, 1967, pp. 15, 328, and passim.
2. See above, p. 12.
3. Fanning the flames of nationalism is the ideological conflict between communists and anticommunists called "the cold war". I have touched on the shaky historical foundations of both ideologies, and the ways the cold war accentuates the overwhelming dangers humanity now faces, in *The United States and Civilization*, pp. 98–110, and in *Conflict Resolution and World Education*, ed. Stuart Mudd, Dr. W. Junk Publishers, The Hague; Indiana University Press, Bloomington, 1966. And the menace of the white versus the colored peoples (as well as that of the cold war) has just been discussed by Lord Boyd Orr (see above, pp. 127, 129 ff.).

who have to think in nationalistic terms, as described by Bourbon Busset and Squirru,[1] is an example of the unreal environment in which people of all countries and in all walks of life now move towards the destruction that few desire. They are blind to the contemporary scientific and technological revolutions.

In treating of culture, Squirru says: "there is no higher national interest than the cultural interest which transcends nationalism." [2] What is true of culture has become true in all realms of endeavor, even national defense. For every nation, arms are now valuable only insofar as they are the instruments of peace. The recently prevalent notion that limited warfare might offer a means of avoiding the all-out battle which few, if any, now in authority are eager to command, rests on a misreading of European history from 1648 to 1789. The "self-generating order," partially established during the times of Hume and Adam Smith, was facilitated by effective sentiment among leaders of thought and policy that all Europe was becoming in spirit a single great republic. Such sentiment hardly prevails as yet on the world stage, which has now become the scene for political decisions. And even in the more homogeneous small world of the eighteenth century, with its increasing distaste for violence and brutality, an important factor in keeping warfare within bounds was the limited *means* for waging it.[3] Today the *means* are hardly limited! As General André Beaufré has recently written, the existence of abundant nuclear weapons has "rendered every kind of military adventure extremely dangerous because of the risks of escalation it involves." He reaches the conclusion that "nuclear armament is properly designed, certainly to prevent nuclear war, but also to prevent all forms of war between the states which possess nuclear weapons." [4]

What of states allied to those with nuclear weapons? Isn't it clear that the only ultimate answer to the new conditions of armament is a guarantee of integral peace, and not limited war?

"To place the national interest above all" has become in consequence, as Maritain recently wrote, "the sure means of losing everything." [5] The patriot of the future will be one who recognizes that his own country stands to gain most if every country, his own included, is provided with opportunities to work out its destiny within its own borders, assisted by

---

1. See above, pp. 92–93, 97.
2. Cf. Nef, *The United States and Civilization*, pp. 48–51.
3. Nef, *War and Human Progress*, esp. pp. 116–17, chap. 13. And cf. chap. 18.
4. *Le Figaro*, August 1, 1966 (my translation).
5. Jacques Maritain, *Le Paysan de la Garonne*, Paris, 1966, p. 105 (my translation).

those negative rules (of which Hayek has spoken and which should now include a denial of the right to make war) as the basic principles behind a spontaneous order extended to the entire world of nations.[1]

The attainment of such an order should not, and need not, be at the expense of national diversity. The North American Union, formed after the Revolution of 1776, has not extinguished the individualism of the thirteen original states or of those territories admitted later to statehood. Now, almost two centuries afterwards, one could hardly claim that a Georgian and a Vermonter are without their particular characteristics. One could only with difficulty claim that a Texan and a citizen of Hawaii are identical in outlook. There has been room, within the self-generating order of an ever larger federal union, for the most diverse sorts of development. The most recent of the newly admitted states, Hawaii, had already as a territory absorbed into its commonwealth not only Hawaiians and whites (mostly of New England origin) but Chinese and Japanese who greatly outnumbered both whites and Hawaiians. Within the Hawaiian Islands there have been no serious national or color barriers to peaceful coexistence, and even, especially in the case of the Chinese and the whites, to happy intermarriage.

It could now be so throughout this planet. National characteristics would remain in countries freed from nationalism, for nationality need not generate those disagreements and conflicts bred of a nationalistic frame of mind.[2] As nation after nation renounced the power of destruction, a world union could gradually form capable of maintaining essentially peaceful relations everywhere.

"It is all very well for idealists like yourselves," we are likely to be told (those of us who hold such views), "to build a dream world for the future without the prejudices and hatreds let loose by nationalism. But under the actual conditions depicted by Bourbon Busset,[3] what country is to be first in adopting a less nationalistic policy?" "Let China or Russia make a substantial gesture;" "Let France make one;" "*Que Messieurs les assassins commencent*" – many in each country will say.

With the possible destructive consequences of nationalism as over-whelming as they are, what is important is not the order of going. What is important is that some nation move at once in the right direction.

Is there a nation better endowed than the United States? For stabilizing

1. Cf. above, pp. 40–42.
2. See above, p. 93 note.
3. See above, pp. 92–94.

national boundaries all over the world, we have a most important tradition which goes back to the founding fathers and to the early days of the Republic. In his remarkably comprehensive and lucid *History of the United States from 1801 to 1817*, Henry Adams shows how uncertain it was, at the start of the nineteenth century, whether the future conquest of North America would lead to union or to division into *several* independent nations. If division had occurred, North America might have become a slaughterhouse, after the pattern so familiar in the ancient Mediterranean and again in Western Europe.

"Peace is our passion," President Jefferson wrote in 1803 [1] to Sir John Sinclair, like Boyd Orr a great Scottish authority on agriculture. It was that passion, for all the terrible Civil War, that brought Lincoln to stand firm sixty years later against secession, and to save the Union.

A half century after that, when the boundaries of the world had greatly shrunk already, Wilson's leadership on behalf of "a war to end war," and his conception of the League of Nations, were a continuation of Jefferson's passion for peace. Wilson was aiming, perhaps only half consciously, to extend to the whole world the union which had saved North America from endless wars. The idea of such a league was of European origin and went back at least to the early seventeenth century,[2] but Wilson's was the first attempt to realize it politically. A republican administration, after repudiating the League, made a half-hearted effort to revive the pacific aspect of Wilson's leadership in the Kellogg-Briand pact calling on all nations to renounce war as an instrument of policy. Roosevelt renewed Wilson's plan as best he could, in the struggle against Germany and Japan, by his support of the new international authority, the United Nations, in which he did not live to participate.

In resuming that peaceful tradition today, the first step would be fundamental changes in the foreign policy the United States has pursued since the Second World War. From 1948 to 1968 we have sought security through an increasingly exclusive dependence on military might. In an age of increasingly unimaginative specialization, we have increasingly put the military specialist and the Department of Defense in the saddle.

Whatever may have been the merits of that policy when it was inaugurated, a creative peace policy has now become the best form of security. In a particular connection, Senator Aiken has recently called for "the wit, the imagination (and) the courage" needed "to devise a political strategy to

1. *Works*, IV, 490, as cited Henry Adams, *History of the United States*, New York, 1931, vol. i, p. 445.
2. Nef, *War and Human Progress*, pp. 142–44.

suit a political problem." Our present resort to "military strength," he suggested, is a device "to hide (our) political ineptitude".[1]

The present policy is fraught with continual frustrations and, in the end, very possibly with self-destruction. World order cannot be *imposed* by any state. For all its material wealth, the United States contains less than a tenth of the world's population. For all its might, it is no match for the rest of the world. Its military commitments are already overextended. Its people have neither the will nor the desire to conquer the earth. The self-generating international order, agreed upon at this meeting as desirable, can come only out of the free adherence of nation after nation to a policy of peace. The policy that is needed is a settlement of all disputes, including our own, through the highly imperfect peacemaking machinery of the United Nations.

As a result of the material transformation of most of the world, all countries would have everything to gain from such a policy. The progress of science and technology has rendered ever less alluring the conquests some Americans feared might be undertaken at the expense of vital United States interests. The two most powerful rival nations (Russia and potentially China) are historically haunted much more by the fear of being invaded than by the wish to conquer. Meanwhile the reasons for the greed Apollinaire considered one cause for war[2] have diminished. "The general level of technological advance (throughout the world) ensures for the first time in human history there can literally be enough to go around – there is no longer any need to kill off the other fellow in order to secure your own individual or group survival".[3] Never before has every nation, large and small, had so rich an opportunity to cultivate its own garden.

We ought not to nourish the illusion, however, that the all-pervasive and largely senseless nationalism would disappear rapidly, even if this new policy of peace were inaugurated. Nor would the violent emotions aroused, not only by communism, but by racial prejudices, which Lord Boyd Orr has discussed.[4] As the explorer and scientist, Vilhjalmur Stefansson, observed some years ago, "man finds it easier to change the face of nature than to change his own mind".[5] We are a long way from an allegiance to

1. *New York Times*, Jan. 20, 1968, pp. 1,4.
2. Cf. above, p. 133.
3. John McHale, Mimeographed Report of Sept. 21, 1965 to Chairmen of ICY Committee on Cultural and Intellectual Exchange.
4. See above, p. 129.
5. Evelyn Stefansson Nef, Introduction to "The Great Explorer Series," in Rhys Carpenter, *Beyond the Pillars of Heracles*, New York, 1966, p. xvii.

the happiness of the individual everywhere, regardless of nationality, economic creed or race, an allegiance which we hope will one day take precedence over nationalism. Meanwhile for decades and even for generations the United States, along with other countries, will be faced by the possibility of sudden failures in a peace policy, and by the forces capable of universal slaughter which such failures could unleash.

Under these conditions, wordly salvation rests to a large extent, as Bourbon Busset has done well to emphasize, on the political leaders at the summit.[1] He stresses the importance of their being men of integrity.

By all means let everything possible be done to bring such men to the summit. Yet, however strong may be the motives of a conscientious leader to avoid the worst, the actual consequences which flow from any decision he is obliged to make in the presence of an either-or choice are highly uncertain. The man at the top often has little or no control over the kind of problem he is called on to settle, or even over the way in which the problem is presented. Certainly this was true of Truman's decision to use the atomic bomb, which has been discussed at length in these pages.

In those ultimate confrontations on which the fate of all human life could now hinge, moreover, the statesman who most wished to avoid total slaughter might miscalculate, for at the point he intervenes he will probably be left without any sure means of accomplishing his wish. Centuries ago a wise and subtle French thinker, Montaigne, in the first of his famous *Essays*, raised the question whether, in the presence of an enemy who seems bent on doing you in, you would stand the best chance of escaping his wrath by putting yourself at his mercy and appealing to his pity, or by threatening to fight back. Montaigne concludes, on the strength of historical examples, that either course may succeed or fail. Indeed the title of this essay, "One attains the same end by diverse means," [2] shows how precarious the unprecedentedly dangerous confrontations of the nuclear age are bound to be.

With the stakes involved in such a situation as Montaigne depicted, now multiplied many million fold, the only real hope for humanity would consist in arranging matters in advance to prevent such confrontations. Of course much of the responsibility for so arranging matters depends upon other prior decisions of the man at the top. But whatever may be the issues that face such a man, does not his capacity to decide them with even a portion of the integral sanity that the nuclear age requires, depend

1. See above pp. 93–95.
2. "Par divers moyens on arrive à pareille fin."

much more than Bourbon Busset's intervention suggests on the state of opinion in his country?

The capacity of the leaders to rise above prevailing opinion *is* considerable. De Gaulle managed to do so in settling France's Algerian war, though on some other issues his soaring independence has been less happy in deflating nationalism! While the President of the United States, to take another example, *has* a most important range of choice, to a not inconsiderable extent he is the prisoner of what appears to be the dominant state of mind at home. He is partly the prisoner of the prevailing prejudices of the bureaucracies which operate the numerous executive branches of government, and whose officials for the most part have been trained as specialists under conditions which have ceased to exist in this age of incredibly rapid material change. He is also partly the prisoner of legislators, many of whom follow what they think are the wishes of uninformed and emotional but vocal constituents, rather than resorting to independent judgments based on permanent values and better information. He can also become a partial prisoner of public opinion polls.

So, to say the least, the capacity of the leader to rise above prevailing opinion and arrange the world for the better is not unlimited! And what if, like Stalin, and even more like Hitler before the Second World War, a leader should personify the evil forces which lurk among the public in every country and which reached an all time low in the Germany which bred the Nazis?

It is consequently not only the men at the top whose values are of concern to a Center for Human Understanding. Edwin Hubble, the great astronomer, was among the first to recognize the complete change in the meaning of war that had resulted from the recent applications of scientific knowledge to destruction. Already in 1946 he called on "*Mankind*" to make choices which would lead "from brute violence to a nobler level of existence." [1]

Every person should be granted an equal *opportunity* in the better society, to which we are trying to contribute in order to achieve a nobler level of existence. But the notion that all humans are equally endowed to make the right choices, that each opinion is of equal value in the realm of general policy (a contention which could hardly be made in connection with a special subject) is likely to lead to the destruction of the very democracy on behalf of which it is often invoked.

The initiative that could enthrone nobler religious, moral, intellectual

---

1. See Nef, *The United States and Civilization*, 2nd ed., p. 412.

and aesthetic values, having a validity for people in every country and revealing the common humanity that transcends nationalism, has to come from individuals. Some of them have to possess the magic [1] to strengthen the will of others who also desire to serve these values, sometimes without the courage to declare themselves.

I am told that Ibsen has one of his characters say: "The minority is sometimes right. The majority is always wrong". I like to think that the deliberations which have found their way into print in this book will help give confidence to those minorities that are capable of working towards the right, always with tolerance, never with force. I like to think the deliberations set forth in these pages will increase the influence of such individuals in policy making, both among the men at the top and with humans wherever authority can count, even in very modest ways, such as in raising families in the home.

Bourbon Busset is mainly right in suggesting that "we can have a rich message for a few people, or a very poor message for great numbers of people." [2] One of the principal obstacles to making the rich message count for the better is the often artificial separation of creative work into watertight compartments. Each specialized subject and realm of endeavor has only its own small public. Already in 1933 Sinclair Lewis remarked "... there are as many sorts of celebrities as there are occupations." [3] So the implications of special discoveries for the welfare of the whole human being are lost.

If the new knowledge and the new achievements are to be brought to bear on the general problems that concern men and women everywhere in the single world this planet has become, it is essential that channels be established where the relations between the special and the general can be examined in their bearing on the goals of civilization.[4] The Center for Human Understanding is a modest effort to provide one such channel. Groups of this kind should be kept small enough so that a dialogue, like the one in these pages, is an expression of the most qualified persons from different occupations who have among themselves close and continuous friendly relations, and whose vision, while deriving nourishment from their specialities, transcends these specialities.

Under existing conditions in most countries, it is only the highest

1. The late Aldous Huxley called them "mystics". See *Gray Eminence*, Harper Colophon edition, New York (1941), 1966, p. 243.
2. See above, p. 91.
3. *Ann Vickers*, New York, 1933, p. 426.
4. Goals I have attempted to formulate (most imperfectly!) in Part II of *The United States and Civilization*, 2nd ed., Chicago, 1967.

governing officials – above all the men at the summit – whose pronouncements on general subjects command a wide audience and so carry the
weight which publicity throws onto the balance. This "summitry" is a
monopoly with dangerous consequences.[1] It overburdens the great decision makers. And it is seldom in the interest of those truths on matters
of general concern – impartially and slowly arrived at in the light of profound thought – which are now so greatly needed for the future of "Mankind". If, therefore, groups that develop after the example of a Center for
Human Understanding can obtain for the wisest pronouncements of their
members an increasing respect and a widening audience, they could offer a
healthy alternative to the present concentration of power.[2] Stimulated by
the interest of young students who are seeking general culture through
their special training,[3] such groups could provide a free market for the
pursuit of truths which have been grievously neglected in the age of the
specialist.

The discussion in Part I of this volume, on the experimental sciences, is
of value especially because it concentrates attention upon the unprecedented problems and dangers with which the discovery and practical uses
of nuclear fission have confronted humanity. But those are not the only
problems the sensational advances in the experimental sciences now
thrust on man. It appears that still more recent developments in biology
may create further bewildering and equally sinister possibilities.[4] How little
has been done to meet both these dangers has been stressed recently by a
distinguished scientist, Dr. Caryl Haskins, President of the Carnegie Institution of Washington. "Too much emphasis cannot be laid," he writes,
"upon the importance of preparing a society to meet such issues long in
advance ..."[5]

The dialogue in the remaining parts of this book, which follow "The
Experimental Sciences," is concerned with meeting these issues. It is concerned with ways of reinforcing the values for which humans at their best
have stood, and which are therefore accessible to the people of all nations
as members of the human family. Researches in the social and behavioral
sciences can reveal much that is helpful to individuals in the conduct of

1. Cf. above, p. 139.
2. See above, p. 131–132. Also "Quelques commentaires sur 4 textes," *Bulletin du Centre
d'Etude des Conséquences Générales des Grandes Techniques Nouvelles* (September 1967).
3. Cf. above, pp. 116 ff.
4. See above, p. 125.
5. *Report of the President of the Carnegie Institution of Washington 1966–1967*, pp. 33–34. See also Bently
Glass, "What are the goals of man's evolution?" (a review of T. Dobzhansky's *The
Biology of Ultimate Concern*) in *Scientific American*, February 1968, pp. 133–36.

their lives, both by warnings and reassurances. This is particularly true if these scientists are conscious of the limitations of their methods and results, and attempt to compensate for the limitations by saturating themselves with at least one of the cultural experiences which are touched upon in the dialogue in Parts III, IV and V.

Here I should like to clarify my view of the issue raised by the interventions of Squirru and Devons following Morazé's paper in Part II. Humanists are, in Squirru's happy phrase, "custodians of the mystery of man." [1] Saying so much does not involve a repudiation of the sciences, as Devons seems to fear.[2] Saying so much involves only the belief, which as an historian I share, that, insofar as meeting the greatest problems that face us today is concerned (including those of world community), the role of any particular science, and even of all sciences taken together, is a limited role.

There remains a place for what is often covered in contemporary language (not very happily) by the term "humanists." As I use it, this term refers to persons who obtain their results in the main by other than scientific methods. Great artists are of that ilk. Though they may to advantage receive a more active training in the technical sides of their work by providing their own materials, their inventions, as distinguished from those of engineers, are governed by the discipline of what Pascal called "the nimbly discerning mind" and are not subject to verification in the same way as scientific results.[3] Historians, who are not bent on making predictions, who do not "gamble on the future," [4] are also of the family of "humanists," as I use the word (although the facts they invoke have to be rigorously verified). So are those who frequent the classics in all the arts and who are interested in consulting the works they study in terms of the conditions under which the subjects were created, without trying to wrench the characters or the scenery, the music or the statues, into molds derived from their own particular environment in time and place.[5] This category of "humanists" also includes, as William Wood Prince emphasizes, persons who effectively practice business diplomacy. As he says, that cannot constructively be governed by "a slide rule." [6]

Devons speaks of physics as being confronted now by deeper problems than those "it has solved".[1] I am not clear whether he means the unprece-

1. See above, p. 47.
2. See above, p. 48.
3. Cf. Nef, *The United States and Civilization*, 2nd ed., pp. 5, 83–84.
4. Cf. above, pp. 89–90.
5. Cf. the trenchant remarks of Marshall Hodgson above, pp. 53 ff.
6. See above, p. 110.
7. See above, p. 49.

dented problems which technological progress, based upon the physical sciences, has presented us all. I am not clear whether he means, in short, those problems of which Haskins writes and which are the occasion for the existence of a Center for Human Understanding. If that is his meaning, then in order to meet such problems, we shall require more than all the experimental sciences and all the human sciences together can supply. If such an independent need for "humanists" be not admitted, then, it would be *scientists* and not humanists who are "repudiating" efforts essential to happiness!

It is an illusion to suppose, for example, that if only researches in the human sciences were helpfully combined with new discoveries in biology, human nature could be changed confidently for the better. There is much evidence historically that the human race, as we now know it, is far from having exhausted its possibilities for religious, moral, intellectual and aesthetic improvement.[1] Have we not still to wager on these possibilities rather than on life created in laboratories?

The evolution of the arts, of education, of the professions and of business enterprise, in the interest of the better sides of our nature, offers the greatest promise of leading humanity "through the barriers of nationalism and ideology" to the community invoked by James Douglas. That is a community "wherein men can coexist not only with mutual benefit, but with mutual confidence and respect." [2]

Thanks partly to the participation of members of the Committee on Social Thought in the dialogue, it is from the realm of higher education (in a wide sense, including the education of artists) that the most constructive suggestions are made in this volume for innovations leading in the direction of such a community. One suggestion is to give a few of the most promising young men and women opportunities to be their best selves in preparing for fresh leadership. In their training, specialization of a new kind, directed towards the discovery of the interrelations between the special and the whole, would help them to find their way.

This search for interrelationships between all lines of endeavor, and all societies, has been opened by both The Committee on Social Thought and the Center for Human Understanding. Out of the search might come constructive ideas for meeting new problems which, for the first time, involve the entire human race as a result of contemporary achievements in the sciences and technologies. That is probably what Lord Boyd Orr has in

---

1. Nef, *The United States and Civilization*, 2nd ed., pp. 106–10.
2. See above, p. 35.

mind, when he speaks of the work initiated by a Center for Human Under-standing as a possible "breakthrough" towards a more peaceful world.[1] We can only hope that we are right in laying our emphasis on this fresh approach to life through works of the mind. We are trying to crossfertilize creative thinking in all lines of intellectual, professional and cultural endeavor, insofar as the thinking is related to universal values that trans-cend every special endeavor and are common to humanity, and insofar as the thinking is directed towards the solution of the new general issues which threaten to destroy mankind. We are trying to give the most dis-interested and wisest thought throughout the world strength it now lacks, overshadowed as it is by the pronouncements of interested persons in positions of political power. In the epoch of Voltaire, Montesquieu, Hume, Kant and Adam Smith, their wise impartial voices were heard and heeded above the pronouncements of heads of state. And in America a leading thinker, hardly less wise than these Europeans, Thomas Jefferson was under President Adams Secretary of State, and then for eight years head of the United States.

In those times the mind helped to bring about the conditions the word "civilization" was coined to describe.[2] The present inconspicuous effort, which has attracted Boyd Orr's attention, might prepare the way for men who can speak with even greater authority than those eighteenth-century giants, on behalf of a future for world civilization under law.

There are, however, serious limits to the results which could be expected from works of the mind, even if Lord Boyd Orr's hopes were fulfilled. Beyond a certain not easily definable point, the pursuit of certainty be-comes a blind alley. Absolute certainty is not of this world. The notion, recently prominent, that all that is needed to put an end to interracial hatred (or for that matter to inter-ideological hatred) is to educate and to feed everyone is over optimistic. I am told that primitive Eskimos, who lack what we call a formal education (though well educated in terms of their own culture) are particularly gentle in their dealings with humans of every kind. Some of the most tender and generous men and women are illiterate. Some of the fiercest and most prejudiced are college graduates, even bearers of the highest degrees. Where are jealousy and suspicious distrust more rampant than among some intellectuals?

The overwhelming need of mankind today is for tolerance, gentleness and mutual understanding among individuals, between races and between

1. See above, pp. 123, 132.
2. Nef, *The United States and Civilization*, 2nd ed., pp. 35–38.

nations. We need to see ourselves as others see us.[1] All need to sympathize with the outlook and even the prejudices, not only of their friends and neighbors, but of the groups and societies they have sometimes been "educated" to treat as enemies. Unless the mind obtains support from the heart for the cause of a single humanity, more effective support than the heart has ever been able to offer before, world community is likely forever to elude "mankind".

What is meant by "the heart?" In his paper concerning the human sciences, Charles Morazé stresses the importance of belief as a means of uniting the billions that today compose the world's population.[2] Belief in what sense? Certainly the great achievements of humans have been founded on profound beliefs. But hitherto all *collective* beliefs – not least among them religious beliefs – have been divisive where the human family as a whole is concerned. They have involved damnation for another segment as the price of salvation for those of one's own faith. Beliefs have thus been the cause of endless bloodshed. The most recent experience with Marxism, related as it has been to the prevalence of communism and anti-communism,[3] does not provide us with the reassurance that strong *beliefs*, unmitigated by compassion, would help in the solution of the problem that brought about this meeting.

At one of our previous meetings, in 1963 in Washington, Marc Chagall said: "It is childish to repeat the truth which has been known so long: In all its aspects the world can be saved only by love." [4] At the same meeting, Mr. S. M. S. Chari (then First Secretary for Education of the Embassy of India in Washington) reported an incident told him by an African diplomat. The diplomat spoke of his brief encounter in the lobby of a big hotel with a small girl of a different color. She was drawn to him (as he was to her) by realizing "that he was also a human being, with the same emotions and the same affection and the same feeling (of love) as any member of her own kith and kin." [5]

The part love might play in encouraging a spontaneous world order has been questioned.[6] Is not the doubt derived from a conception of the meaning of love different from the one intended by Chagall and Chari and also by Dr. Evans? [7] When the value of love as a unifying element is questioned,

1. Nef (ed.) *Bridges of Human Understanding*, New York, 1964, pp. 15 ff.
2. See above, p. 44.
3. Cf. Nef, *The United States and Civilization*, 2nd ed., pp. 98 ff.
4. *Bridges of Human Understanding*, p. 120.
5. *Ibid.*, pp. 90–91.
6. See above, p. 42.
7. See above, p. 31.

it is because the meaning given the word is restricted to pleasure that is basically selfish. In that sense love is perishable. It can be of little help in bringing about world order.

But *self*-love is the opposite of love, as Saint-Exupéry and others before him have told us. Of course no human is capable of the total renunciation to which faith enjoins us in the admonition to love God for Himself and one's neighbor for God. Nor is it possible, or perhaps even desirable, in conjugal love to lose oneself altogether in the other. But the love which I assume Dr. Evans had in mind when he intervened in this meeting is an overwhelming affection, and even devotion, which lifts a man (or a woman) out of himself (or herself), out of the egocentric pre-occupations which often poison their lives. That love makes life almost infinitely precious. A supreme value is conferred on the renewal, in an uninterrupted cycle, of births and deaths.

Each human being is, in varying degrees, a bundle of imperfections. Yet, as Morazé says, "the human body ... constitutes the only positive reality ... common to all ..." [1] The capacity it acquires by love to rise beyond the self confers a dignity on the body which cannot desert its custodian. Consequently he cannot remain indifferent to the virtually total destruction of human life. Now that the threat of such destruction is real, is it realistic to reject love as a guide along the road which could lead men and women towards world community?

1. See above, p. 45.

APPENDIX

THE FUTURE OF A CENTER FOR HUMAN UNDERSTANDING

The value of some of the suggestions which have emerged from meetings of this Center is beginning to be recognized among a widening circle of persons acquainted with the work carried on during the past ten years, especially since the first plenary meeting held in Washington in 1962. These suggestions are at the disposal of any persons who wish to make use of them.[1] Some may perhaps be impelled, as Lord Boyd Orr hopes, to form groups similar to the Center in many parts of the world. We like to think that we might possibly have in the formation of such groups the beginnings of a world university, which should be something very different from a replica, on a large scale, of existing national universities.

This suggestion is made without prejudice to the *altogether separate proposals* for a university of the World Academy of Art and Science.[2] The Center for Human Understanding is and will remain an entirely independent group. The American Division of the World Academy has generously published *TOWARDS WORLD COMMUNITY* under its auspices, but the Academy[3] was in no way serponsible for the meeting held by the Center in 1966, nor is it in any way responsible for the editing of this book.

The idea of a world university, as brought forward repeatedly at meetings of the Center for Human Understanding, (see documents 1-6 listed below) is the Center's own.

It was partly with a view to disseminating ideas discussed at its meetings since 1958, and to enlarging these ideas in the light of developments on the

1. See below, p. 152.
2. See WAAS, Vol. IV, Appendix. pp. 292-310.
3. Of which Lord Boyd Orr is Honorary President and the editor a member. But it was not as members of the Academy that we participated in the Chicago meeting.

world stage, that the John and Evelyn Nef Foundation was established in 1964 and qualified for tax exemption under the provisions of the United States Internal Revenue Code. The functions of the Center as it has existed since 1958 will soon be taken over by that Foundation, of which I am President and my wife is Treasurer.[1] It used to be the custom to grant leases for lives. Insofar as active work for the ends pursued by the Center are concerned, the lease of the Nef Foundation is for at least two lives, for my wife is considerably younger than I am.

The headquarters of the Foundation will be at the same address where the Center was finally established in 1965, at *2726 N Street, N.W., Washington, D.C. 20007, U.S.A.* All inquiries and proposals should be addressed there. Persons interested in the work which has already been done can obtain, by writing to us at that address, published and unpublished documents which the Center has issued, including this volume. (Information concerning our future activities can be obtained in the same way.)

A list of some of the documents is appended, together with a list of those persons who have been, since its inception, members of the Center for Human Understanding. Their support has taken a variety of forms. Without the nourishment I obtained from their interest, it would not have been possible for me to undertake an assignment for which I believe there is an overwhelming need.

> John Nef, Chairman
> Center for Human Understanding
> 2726 N Street, N.W.
> Washington, D.C. 20007 U.S.A.

DOCUMENTS OF A CENTER FOR HUMAN UNDERSTANDING

(Please send postage, and, in the case of printed books, please send a check or money order to cover the price.)

1. "Higher Education and Leadership," John Nef
2. "A New Conception of Grandeur," (Proceedings of the plenary meeting of 1962 in Washington.)
3. *Bridges of Human Understanding*, New York 1964, price $ 6. (Proceedings of the plenary meeting of 1963 in Washington.)
4. "Educational Reform and the Future of the Human Race," John Nef
5. "Origin and History of the Formation of a Center for Human Understanding," John Nef
6. *Towards World Community*, The Hague, 1968, price $ 3.50 (Proceedings of the plenary meeting of 1966 in Chicago.)

1. The other officers are Robert C. Carswell, of New York, Vice-President, and Thomas H. Alcock, of Chicago, Secretary.

MEMBERS OF A CENTER FOR HUMAN UNDERSTANDING

John Nef (Chairman)
Jacques Maritain (Honorary)
Thomas Hoban Alcock
Herbert L. Anderson
Charles Benton
William Benton
Jacques de Bourbon Busset
Thomas H. Carroll (d.1964)
Mrs. William R. Castle
Marc Chagall
Kenneth Dam
Jean Désy (d.1960)
James H. Douglas

Mircea Eliade
Mrs. Max Epstein (d. 1968)
Friedrich A. Hayek
Louis Leprince-Ringuet
Ludwig Mies van der Rohe
Ralph J. Mills, Jr.
Charles Morazé
William Wood Prince
Jean Sarrailh (d.1964)
André Siegfried (d.1959)
Mr. and Mrs. Alfred Shaw
Hermon Dunlap Smith

OTHER SUPPORTERS

Hugo Anderson
Mrs. John V. Farwell III
Marshall Field (d.1965)
Daggett Harvey
Evelyn S. Nef

Bruce Phemister
Rafael Squirru
James Stricklin
Eleanore Wood Prince